75 MORE IRISH SESSION TUNES
FOR ANGLO CONCERTINA

GARY COOVER
WITH
ERNESTINE HEALY

Rollston Press

75 More Irish Session Tunes for Anglo Concertina
by Gary Coover with Ernestine Healy

All rights reserved. No part of this book may be reproduced, scanned, transmitted or distributed in any printed or electronic form without the prior permission of the author except in the case of brief quotations embodied in articles or reviews.

Copyright © 2024 Gary Coover

ISBN-13: 978-0-9970748-7-1

All titles are in the public domain unless otherwise noted.

Cover photo courtesy of Randal Bays, Director of the Ceol Cascadia Irish Music Association Annual Cascadia Irish Music Week (www.ceolcascadia.org).

Also by Gary Coover: *75 Irish Session Tunes for Anglo Concertina* (Rollston Press, 2015)

ROLLSTON PRESS
1717 Ala Wai Blvd, Suite 1703
Honolulu, HI 96815
www.rollstonpress.com

TABLE OF CONTENTS

INTRODUCTION 5
KEYBOARD AND TABLATURE 6
SESSIONS AND ETIQUETTE 7

REELS
Ashplant, The 11
Bank of Ireland 12
Castle Kelly 13
Concertina Reel 14
Cup of Tea 15
Farewell to Ireland 16
Glass of Beer 18
Green Fields of America 19
High Reel 20
Humours of Tulla 21
Maid of Mount Kisco 22
Miss Monaghan 23
Morning Dew 24
Music in the Glen 25
Musical Priest 26
Old Concertina Reel 27
Old Torn Petticoat 28
Over the Moor to Maggie 29
Paddy Fahey's #1 30
Pigeon on the Gate 31
Rakish Paddy 32
Scholar, The 33
Ships Are Sailing 34
Silver Spire 35
St. Anne's Reel 36
Star of Munster 37
Swallowtail Reel 38
Swinging on a Gate 39

JIGS and SLIDES
Behind the Haystack 43
Brosna Slide 44
Coleraine 45
Dennis Murphy's Slide 46
Dingle Regatta 47
Maid in the Meadow 48
O'Keefe's Slide 49
Orphan, The 50
Rakes of Kildare 51
Saddle the Pony 52
Ship in Full Sail 53

Sixpenny Money 54
Smash the Windows 55
Star Above the Garter 56
Swallowtail Jig 57
Tenpenny Bit 58
Tobin's Favorite 59
Top of Cork Road (Father O'Flynn) 60
Trip to Sligo 61

SLIP JIGS
Drops of Brandy 65
Fig for a Kiss 66
Foxhunter's Jig 67

HORNPIPES
Bantry Bay 71
Flowing Tide, The 72,73
Harvest Home 74
Kitty's Wedding 75
Love Will You Marry Me 76
Off to California 77
Walsh's Hornpipe 78

POLKAS
Ballydesmond #2 81
John Egan's 82
Little Diamond 83
Mairi's Wedding 84
Murroe Polka 85
Riding on a Load of Hay 86
Terry Teahan's 87
Tom Sullivan's 88

AIRS
Blind Mary (Mhaire Dhall) 91,92
Inisheer 93
Londonderry Air 94
Minstrel Boy 95
Ned of the Hill 96

SET DANCES, WALTZES, ETC.
Irish Mazurka, The 99
Killavil Postman 100
Parnell's March 102
Planxty Charles Coote 104
Planxty Irwin 105
South Wind 106

THE AUTHORS 107
ALPHABETICAL LIST 108

75 More Irish Session Tunes for Anglo Concertina

INTRODUCTION

By popular demand, here are 75 *more* favorite Irish Session tunes with easy-to-learn play-by-number tablature specifically written for the 30-button C/G Anglo concertina.

This second book features the professional assistance of Ernestine Healy, one of Ireland's top concertina players. She has personally checked the notations and recommended the buttons based on her years of experience and innate familiarity with the Irish musical tradition.

It's been said you can't learn Irish music from "the dots", and there's a certain amount of truth to that. It's a quick way to learn notes and their locations on your instrument, but then you need to get past the mechanics to learn the proper feeling, dynamics, and rhythm.

Although there are probably 400-500 tunes in the basic Irish session repertoire, this book along with 75 *Irish Session Tunes for Anglo Concertina* (Rollston Press, 2015) will get you well on your way to being able to participate in most Irish music sessions. Just remember that favorite tunes vary from session to session, and different groups will often play different variations of the same tune.

Like its predecessor, this book is written for 30-button Anglo concertinas that have the "Wheatstone/Lachenal" system of accidentals on the top row of the righthand side (as opposed to the "Jeffries" accidental layout). Most professional Irish concertina players play instruments with Jeffries accidentals since they have a high c# note in both directions. But Anglos with the Wheatstone/ Lachenal accidentals are the most common, so this book is for those players who still want to be able to play their favorite traditional Irish tunes.

Don't worry if you don't read music – this book utilizes a simple tablature system that will get you playing even the most basic tunes very quickly. Every tune also includes a simple Button Map graphic showing you exactly which buttons are needed to play that particular tune.

Due to the Anglo having so many alternate notes in different directions, there are many ways to play the tunes in this book. The tablature shows one way, but it's not the only way. Various players will have different favorite button choices, and there is no right or wrong way as long as you can play the tune with the appropriate rhythm and flow and speed. It's up to you to learn, experiment, and find your best and most musical way to play a particular tune.

Once you have learned the basic tunes you can begin to experiment with ornamentation, a key component of Irish traditional music. To be used sparingly, like adding spices to your favorite dish, they can lift and enhance your playing and give it energy and lilt.

After learning these new tunes through tablature, you might be able to start reading standard musical notation directly, or learning by ear, and can figure out on your own which buttons and directions work best. If so, this will open up the larger world of Irish traditional music.

Slainte!

KEYBOARD AND TABLATURE

This the button numbering system for the 30-button Anglo concertinas in the key of C/G:

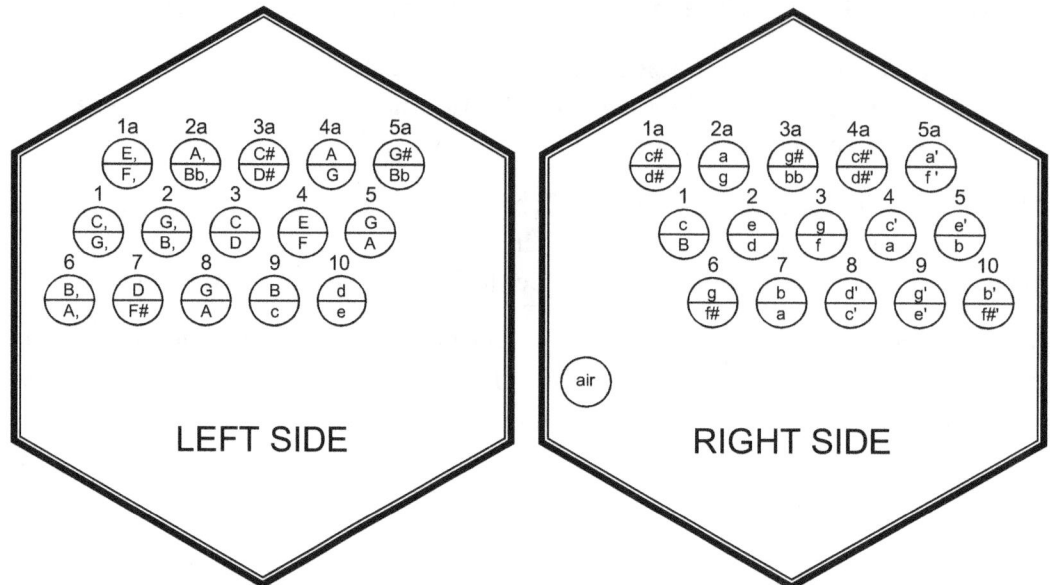

Low notes are on the left side of the instrument and high notes are on the right. Notes shown above the line are on the push, notes shown below the line are on the pull. Standard abc notation has been used to show the pitches of the notes.

How the tablature works in this book:

- The buttons are numbered using the "1a-10" numbering system for each side.
- Buttons on the right-hand side are shown above the musical notes.
- Buttons on the left-hand side are shown below the musical notes.
- Notes on the push are shown by button number only.
- Notes on the pull are shown by button number with a line across the top.
- Long phrases all on the pull will have one long continuous line above the button numbers.
- Notes that are held longer indicated with dashed lines after the button number.

EXAMPLE:

Each tune also has a Button Map showing the buttons needed to play that particular tune:

Buttons played

SESSIONS AND ETIQUETTE

The Irish Music Session as we know it today is actually a fairly recent development, dating only to the 1950's and maybe the 1930's. The tunes of course are much older and were typically played solo for personal entertainment or to accompany dancers at house parties.

Today's typical Irish Session is an informal private or public gathering of musicians who play traditional Irish music together as a group. Sessions are usually open to anyone to join in provided they already know how to play the tunes and can keep up with the pace. Some sessions are only for virtuoso players, others cater to beginners. Sometimes the core group has been hired by pub management with others allowed in by invitation only.

Every session is different – some have great "craic", some are deadly serious, some are furiously fast, and some are "Slow Sessions" geared specifically toward learners. In some sessions musicians take turns going around the circle to start tunes, in others they just jump in.

Irish sessions are not free-for-all "jam sessions", so don't even think about bringing bongos or saxophones. The focus is on Irish Traditional Music with traditional instruments. Every session operates differently, with different rules and conventions, so be respectful and aware.

Session styles vary from place to place and all seem to have different unwritten guidelines. It's much better to observe first before barging in. But don't take a seat in the inner circle unless you are going to play. And don't bring sheet music unless it's a beginner session that allows it.

Most tunes are played more quickly than for Irish dancing, and it is fairly standard for tunes to be grouped together in sets with each tune played two or three times before going into the next tune with no warning. Unlike Bluegrasss music sessions, there are no "breaks" where one musician will go off on some jazz-infused variation while everyone else plays rhythm. For Irish music it's everyone playing all at once, all the time, very straightforward.

Since one of the unwritten rules is "only play tunes that you know", hopefully this book will give you a good head start. Many sessions look down on those who can't play fast enough, or if they just "noodle around" trying to fake their way through the tune.

Please remember that concertinas can be very loud – since the sound blows out each end anyone next to you will hear it much louder than you do. Be mindful of this and respectful to others within earshot.

Although it's tempting, do not sit next to any other concertina players! Since you hear them louder than you hear yourself, you'll end up playing much louder in order to hear yourself. But worst of all, if either makes a mistake, the other then might unknowingly correct, which of course is a bigger mistake, the first one then corrects, making more mistakes, and it can all go downhill really fast from there.

If playing in a group or music session, strive to blend in rather than dominate. You want to be invited back again, right? Shine when appropriate, but blending in is the key to good music and good relations at a typical Irish session.

Important Things to Remember

- Irish tunes can be known by many different names.
- Tunes often have local and regional variations.
- Learning from "the dots" is no substitute for learning with your ears.
- Study the rhythm, lilt and feel of the tune first.
- Sheet music cannot teach style.
- Notation is only an approximation of one version.
- Tablature is a crutch to help you get started.
- Button numbers are suggestions, not absolutes.
- Always try to have an extra finger available for the next note.
- Minimize bellows reversals for faster playing.
- Rhythm and phrasing are more important than speed.
- Use buttons and bellows to breathe life into the tune.
- Play music, don't just push buttons.
- And most important of all, enjoy what you are playing!

REELS

An "ashplant" is an Irish walking stick made from the sapling of an ash tree.

Buttons played

The Ashplant

Traditional

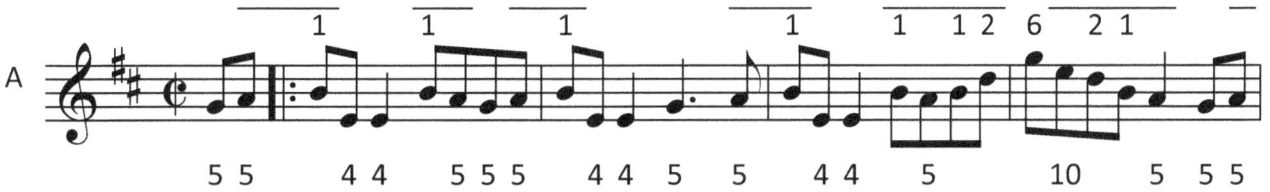

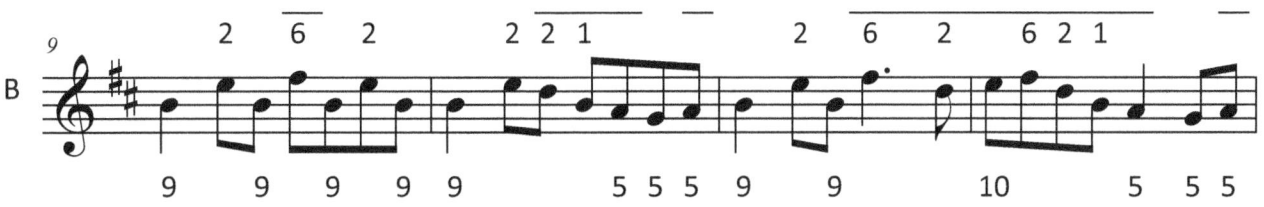

Transcribed from a fiddle manuscript by Francis Reynolds of Gaigue, County Longford, c.1885 where he titled it "Follow Me Down to Carlow". The current title is likely named for the Bank of Ireland building on College Green in Dublin, former home of the Irish Parliament.

Buttons played

Bank of Ireland

Traditional

The O'Kelly's had lots of castles, so this is very likely named after at least one of them.

Buttons played

Castle Kelly

Traditional

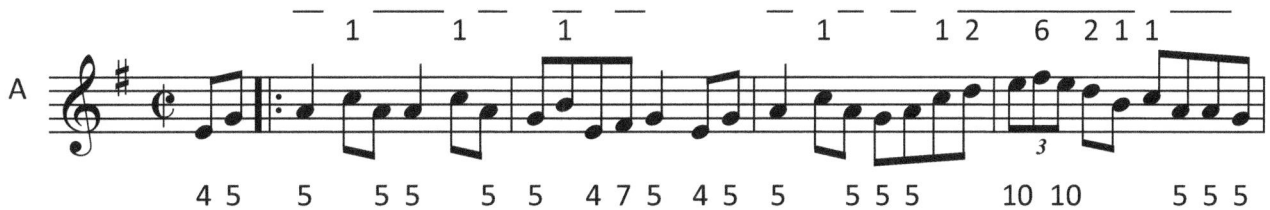

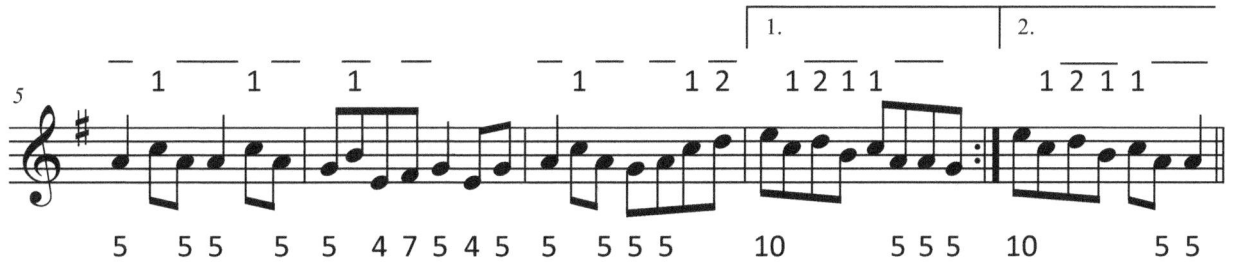

From the concertina playing of Ellen Killeen from Enistymon, and originally played by her son, piper Willie Clancy, in the key of G.

Buttons played

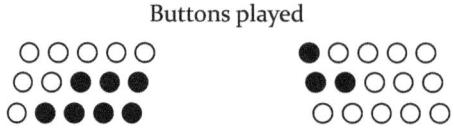

The Concertina Reel

Traditional

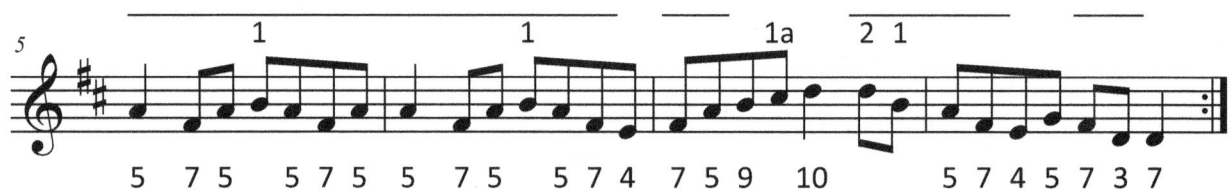

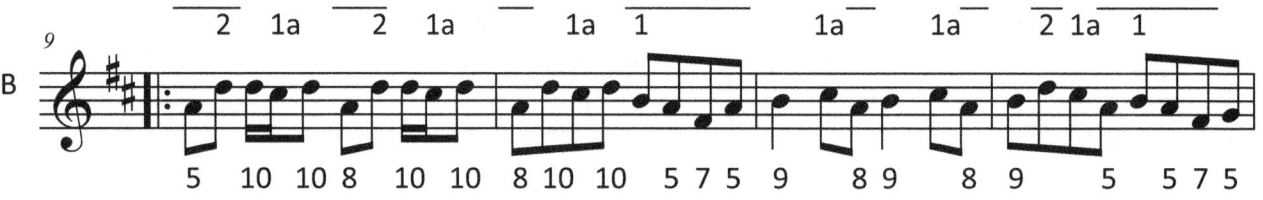

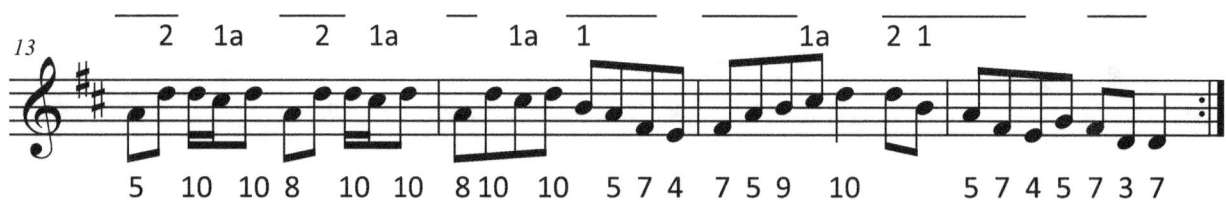

Originally known as "The Unfortunate Cup of Tea." Unfortunately, the story behind the name has been lost.

Cup of Tea

Published by O'Neill in *O'Neill 1001: The Dance Music of Ireland* in 1907, and first recorded by Frank O'Higgins in 1938.

Buttons played

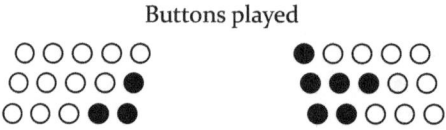

Farewell to Ireland

Traditional

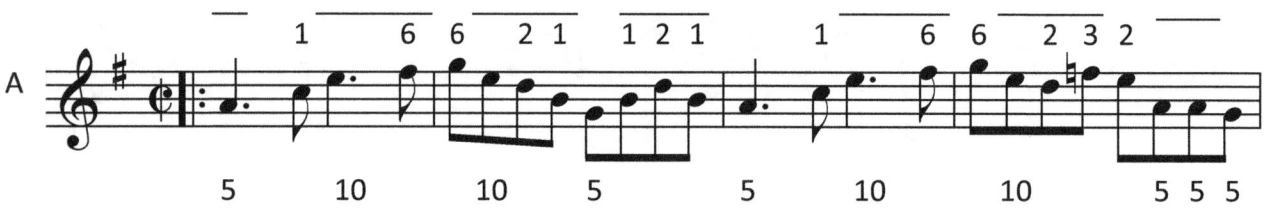

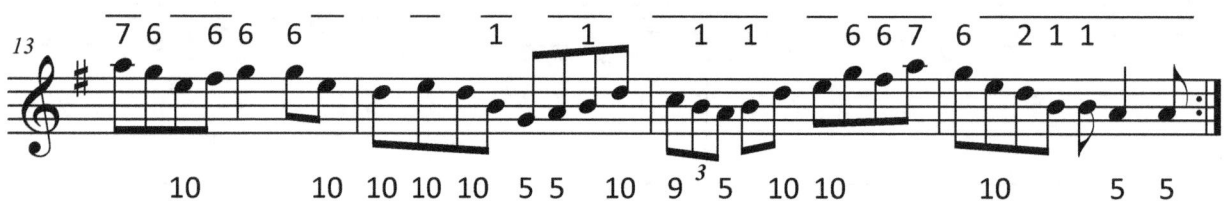

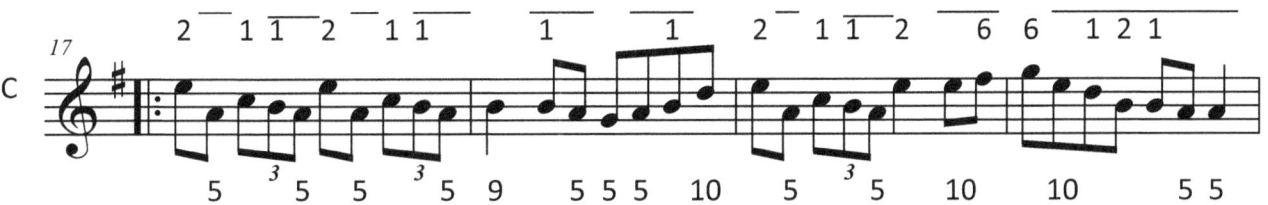
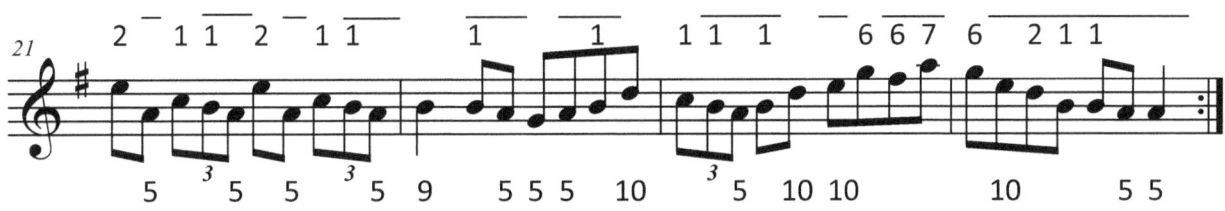
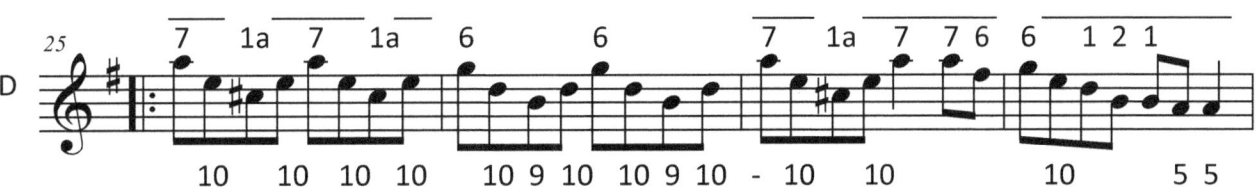
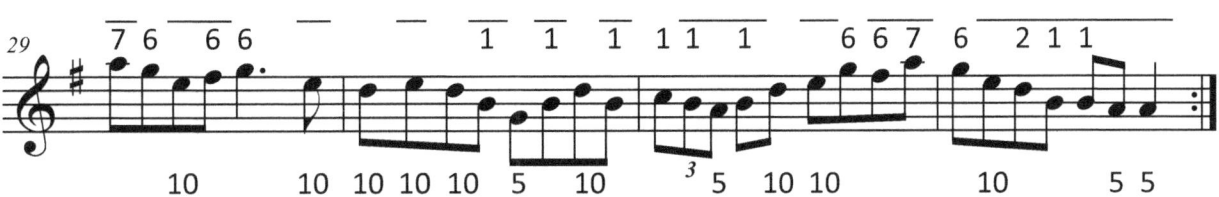

Perhaps composed by John McFadden, a contemporary of Captain Francis O'Neill.

Buttons played

Glass of Beer

Traditional

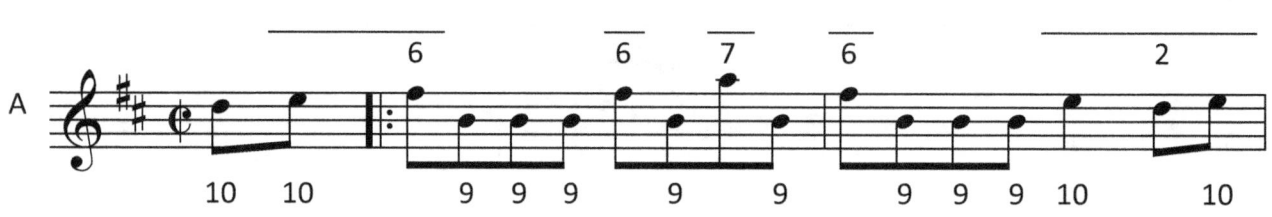

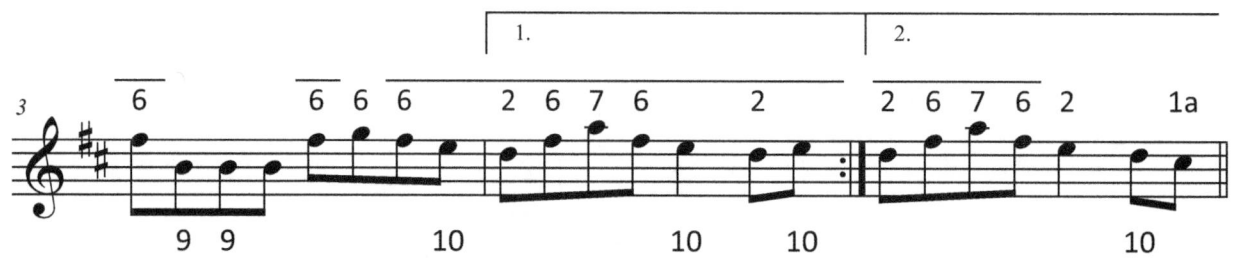

This reel was first published in London in the 19th century, and is also found in a c. 1840's manuscript collection belonging to New York painter and fiddler William Sydney Mount.

Buttons played

The Green Fields of America

Traditional

75 More Irish Session Tunes for Anglo Concertina

This tune might have originated in Scotland as "Sandy Duff", and was printed in O'Neill's as "Duffy the Dancer".

Buttons played

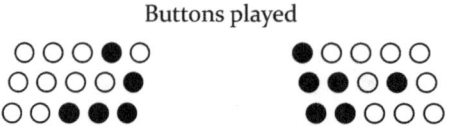

The High Reel

Traditional

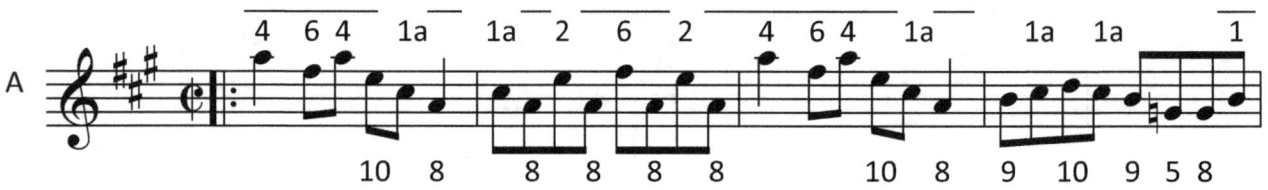

20   75 More Irish Session Tunes for Anglo Concertina

The town of Tulla is in County Clare, just east of Ennis, and is the home of a the Tulla Ceili Band.

Buttons played

Humours of Tulla

Traditional

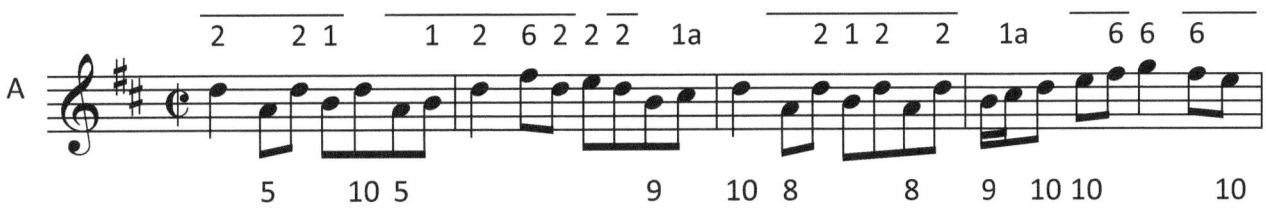

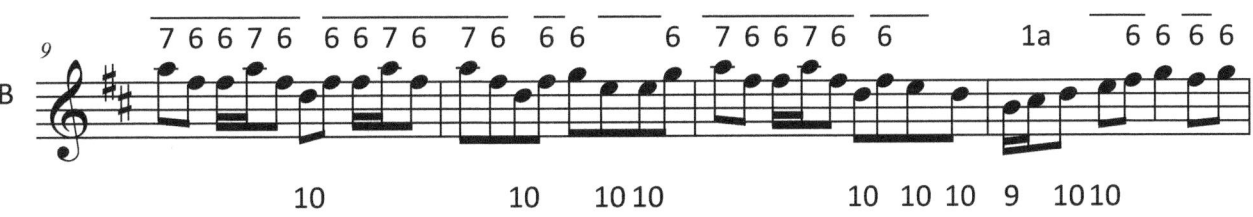

This tune was reportedly composed by Sligo fiddler Paddy Killoran and named for his friend Ann Mulligan from the town of Mt. Kisco in Westchester County, New York. It was first recorded by Killoran in 1937.

Buttons played

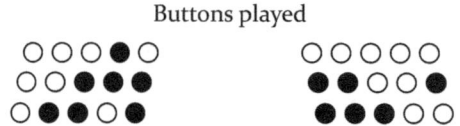

Maid of Mount Kisco

Traditional

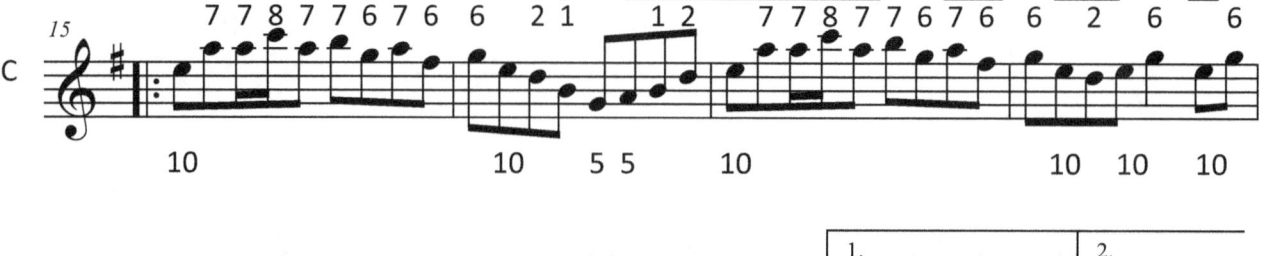

This tune first appears in a mid-19th manuscript collection and was first recorded by uilleann piper Patsy Touhey on home cylinder recordings made by Captain Francis O'Neill c.1902-1904.

Miss Monaghan

Traditional

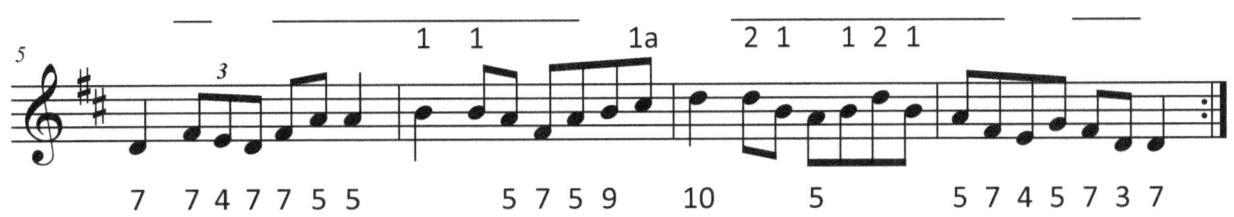

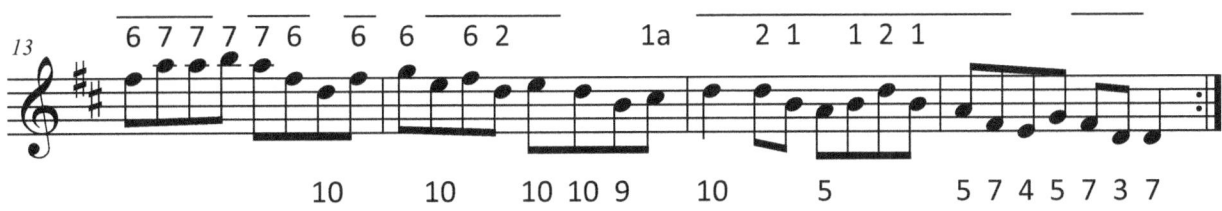

First printed in Scotland in the 1880's as "The Hare Among The Heather" and popularized by The Chieftains as "The Morning Dew".

Morning Dew

Traditional

Known to many from the 1976 Bothy Band album *Old Hag You Have Killed Me*, this tune was also famously recorded by Irish fiddler Martin Wynne in 1950.

Buttons played

Music in the Glen

Traditional

First published in 1865 as "The New Bridge of Eden", it has also been called "The New Bridge of Erin", and is called "Musical Priest in the 1903 *Music of Ireland: 1850 Melodies by O'Neill*. It was recorded by fiddler James Morrison in 1935.

Buttons played

The Musical Priest

Traditional

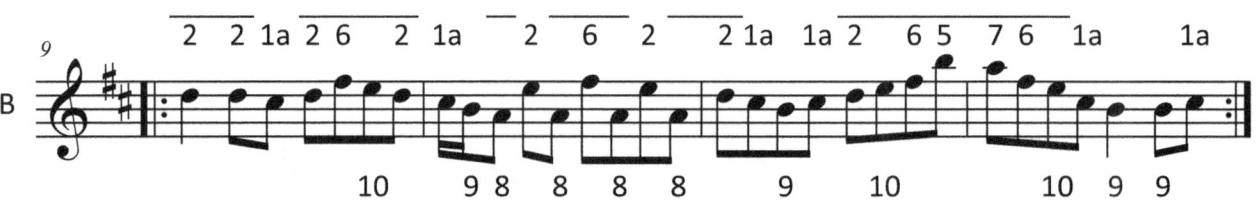

26   75 More Irish Session Tunes for Anglo Concertina

From the concertina playing of Niall Valley.

Buttons played

The Old Concertina Reel

Traditional

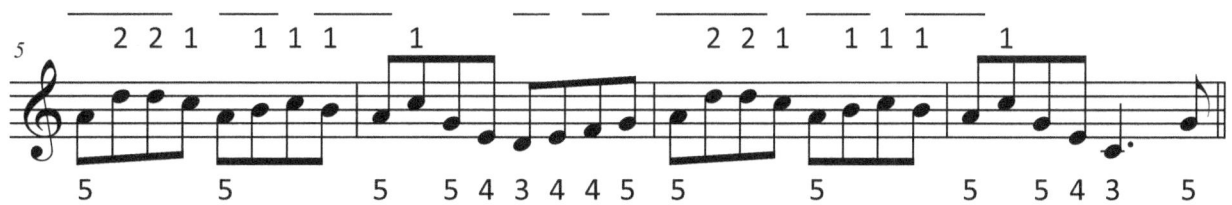

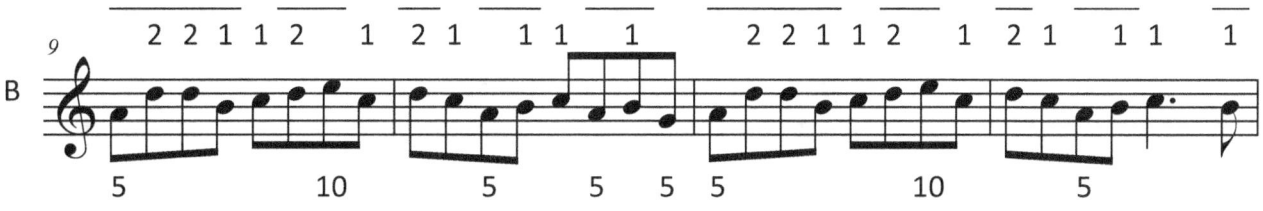

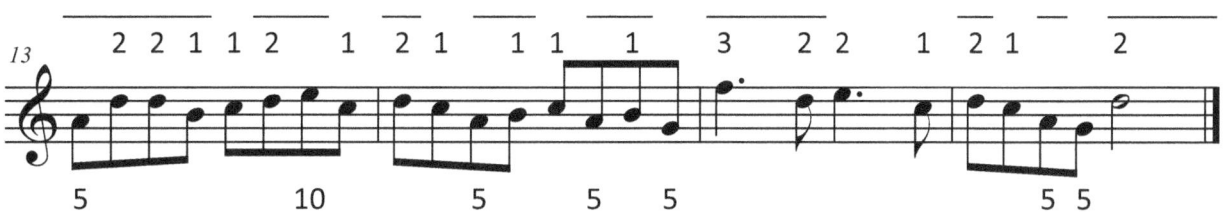

Also called "The Old Torn Petticoat I Got in Mullingar", this tune was first recorded in 1924.

The first two parts of this tune were first published in 1858, with the third part appearing in the 1907 edition of O'Neill's *Dance Music of Ireland*.

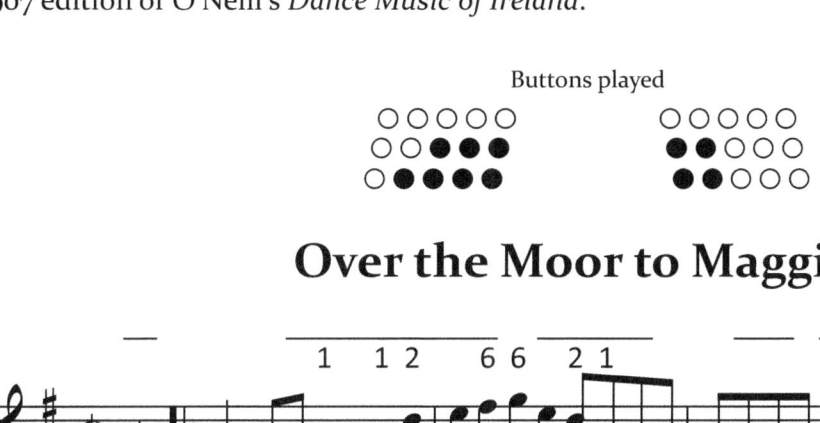

Over the Moor to Maggie

Traditional

75 More Irish Session Tunes for Anglo Concertina

One of many wonderful tunes composed by fiddler Paddy Fahey from Kilconnell in East Galway.

Buttons played

Paddy Fahey's Reel #1

Paddy Fahey

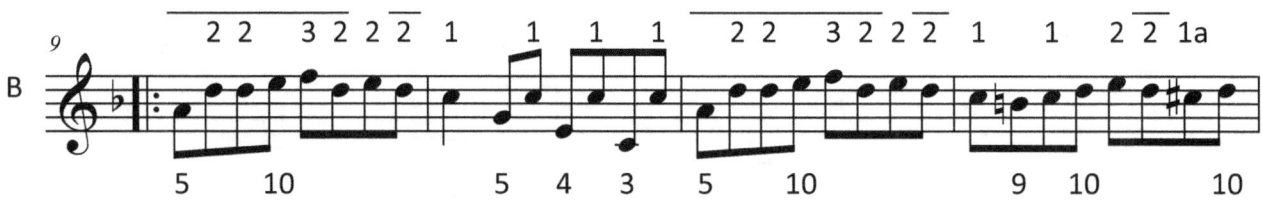

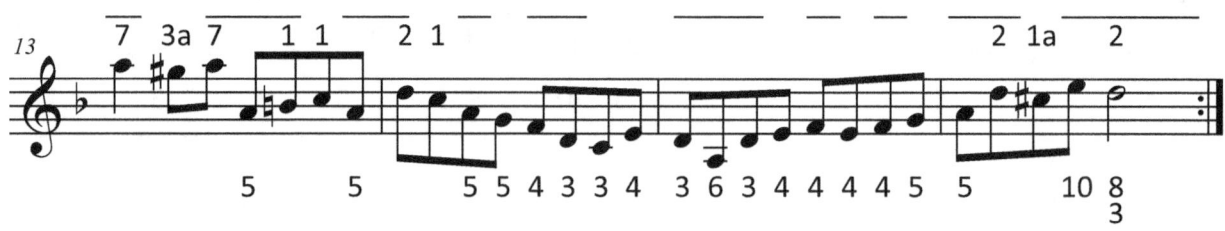

A popular piping tune that most likely originated from the south and west of Ireland in the 1800's.

Buttons played

The Pigeon on the Gate

Traditional

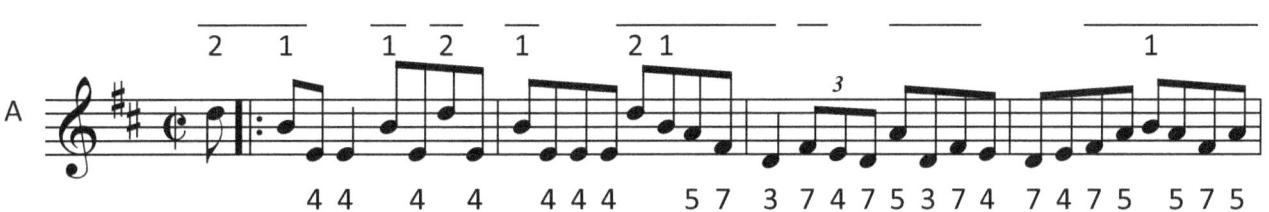

First published in Scotland in 1768 as "Caper Fey" (The Deer's Horns). Michael Coleman later added two additional parts to the tune.

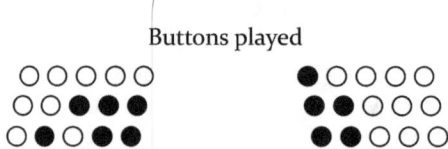

Rakish Paddy

Composed by fiddler James Hill and listed as a hornpipe in O'Neills "Music of Ireland", it is more commanly played today as a reel.

The Scholar

Traditional

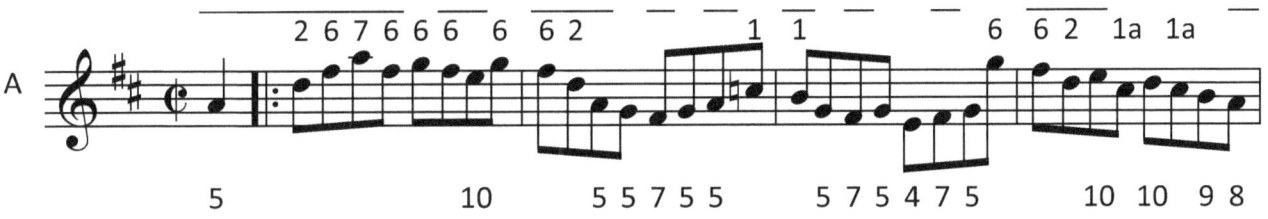
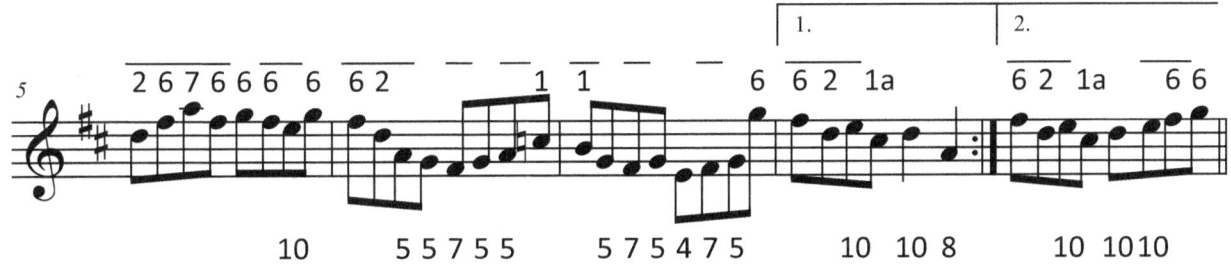

First published by Captain O'Neill in 1903 and recorded in 1924 by Peter Conlon.

Buttons played

Ships Are Sailing

Traditional

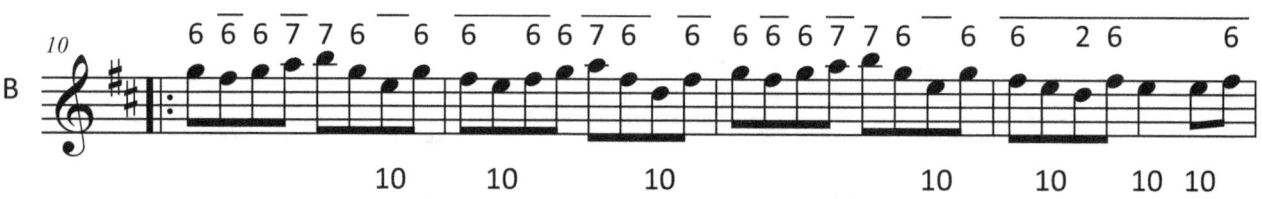

In *Ryan's Mammoth Collection* (1883) this tune is called the "Great Eastern Reel", likely named for famous a transatlantic steamship. The name "Silver Spire" comes from a 1931 recording by Paddy Killoran and Paddy Sweeney and might refer to the Chrysler Building in New York.

Buttons played

The Silver Spire

Traditional

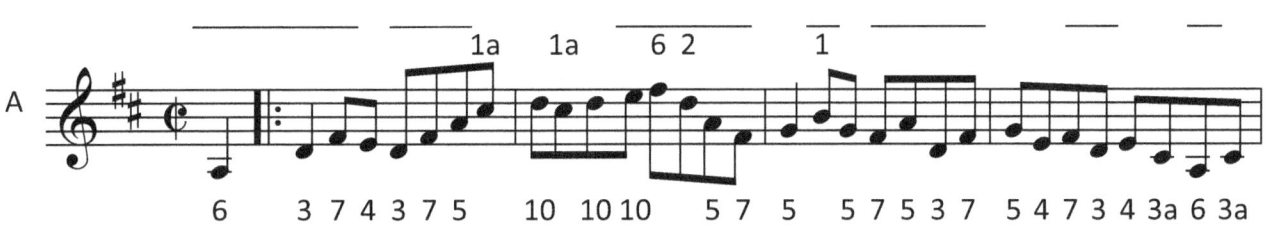

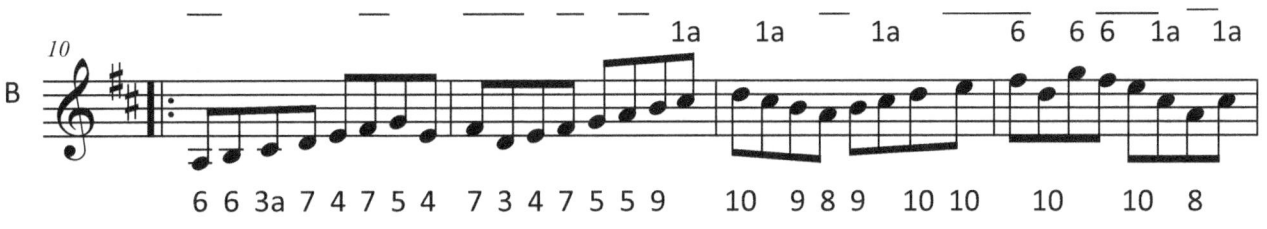

First recorded by Quebec fiddler Joseph Allard as "Reel de Ste Anne", this is a popular tune in Canada, America and also in Ireland, often with variations. This version is quite different from the one usually played by American oldtime musicians.

Buttons played

St. Anne's Reel

Traditional

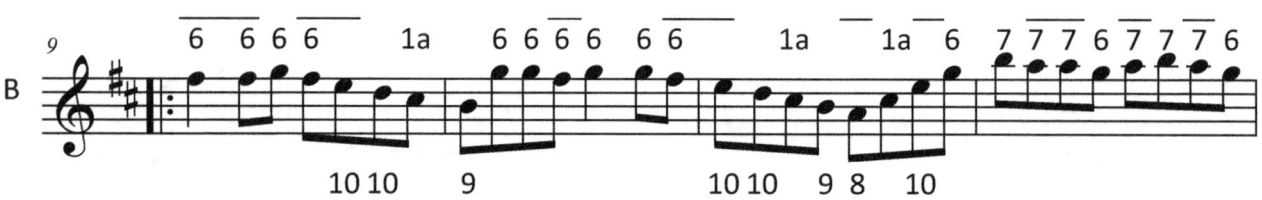

First published by Captain O'Neill in 1903 and first recorded by John Kimmel in 1916.

Buttons played

Star of Munster

Traditional

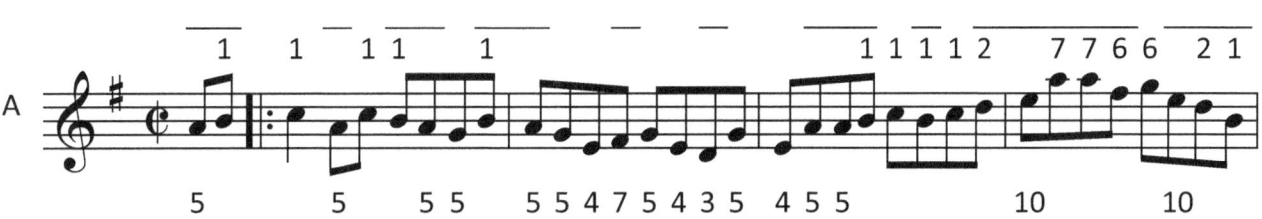

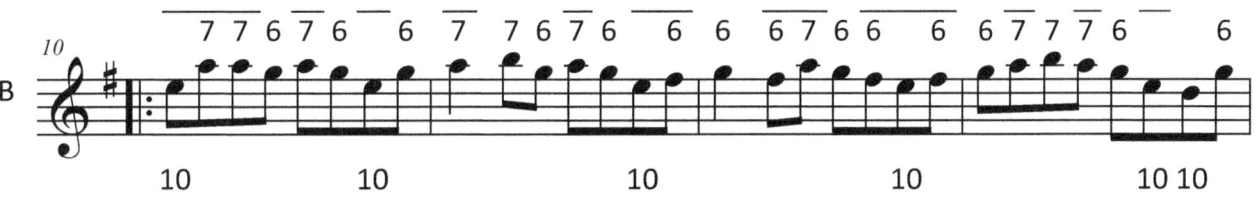

Called "The Swallow's Tail" in the 1903 O'Neill's "Music of Ireland" and first recorded in 1904 by John McFadden.

Swallowtail Reel

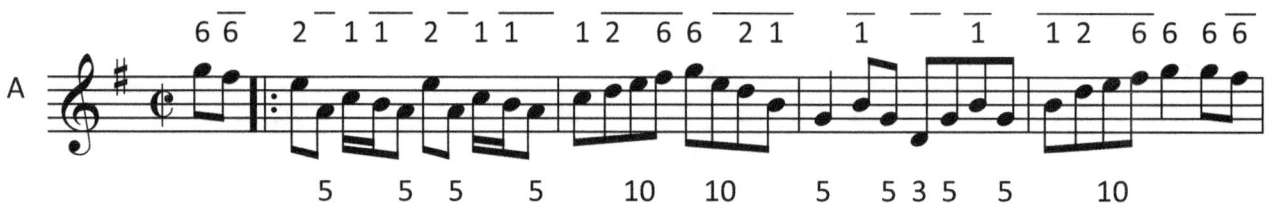
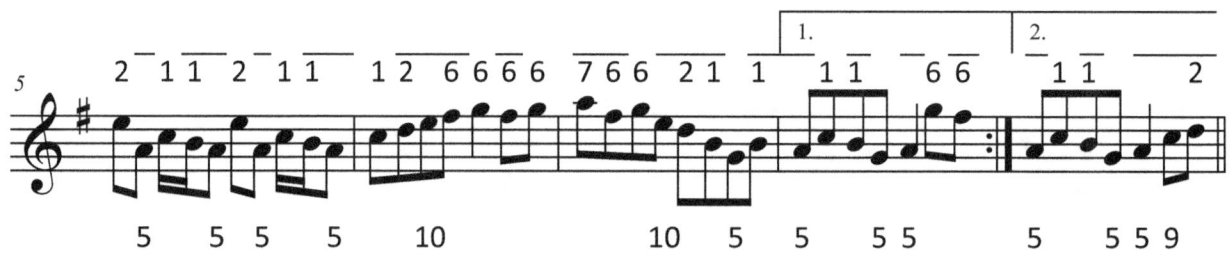
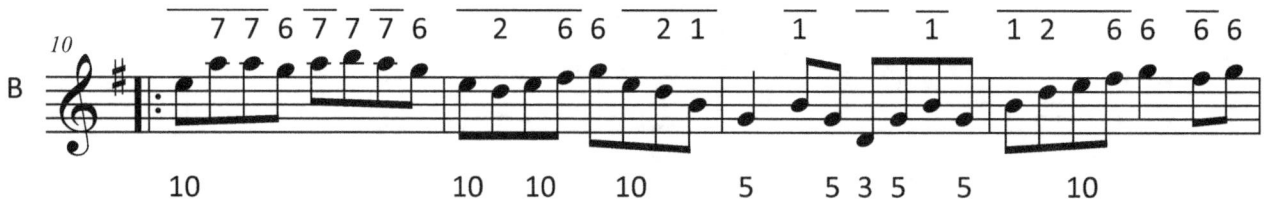

This tune is also a very popular for New England contradances.

Swinging on a Gate

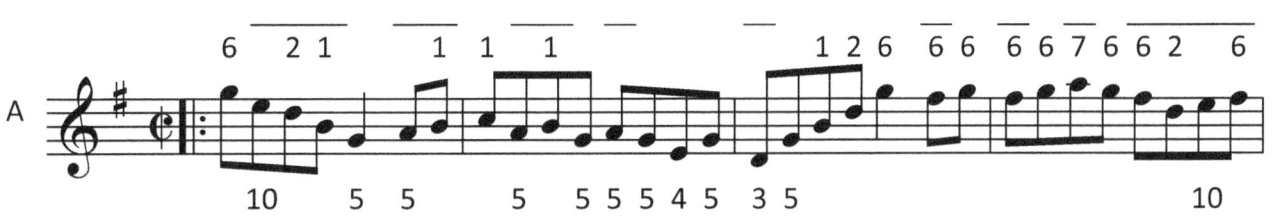

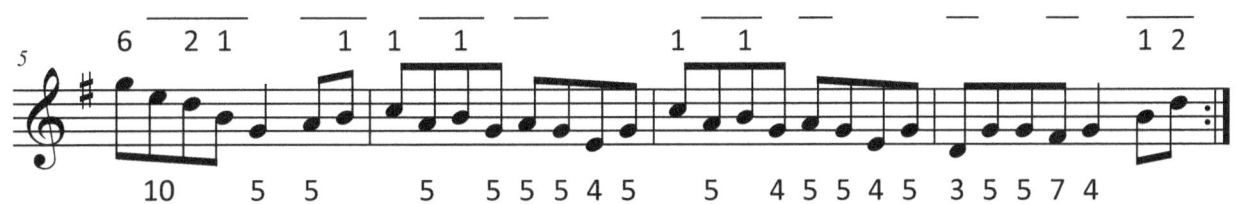

Jigs and Slides

This three-part jig was called "The Munster Buttermilk" by Uilleann piper Seamus Ennis.

Buttons played

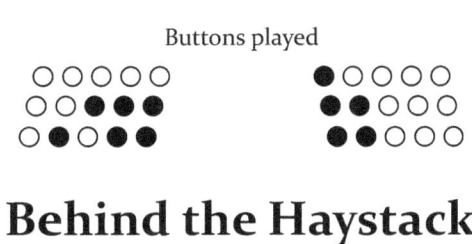

Behind the Haystack

Traditional

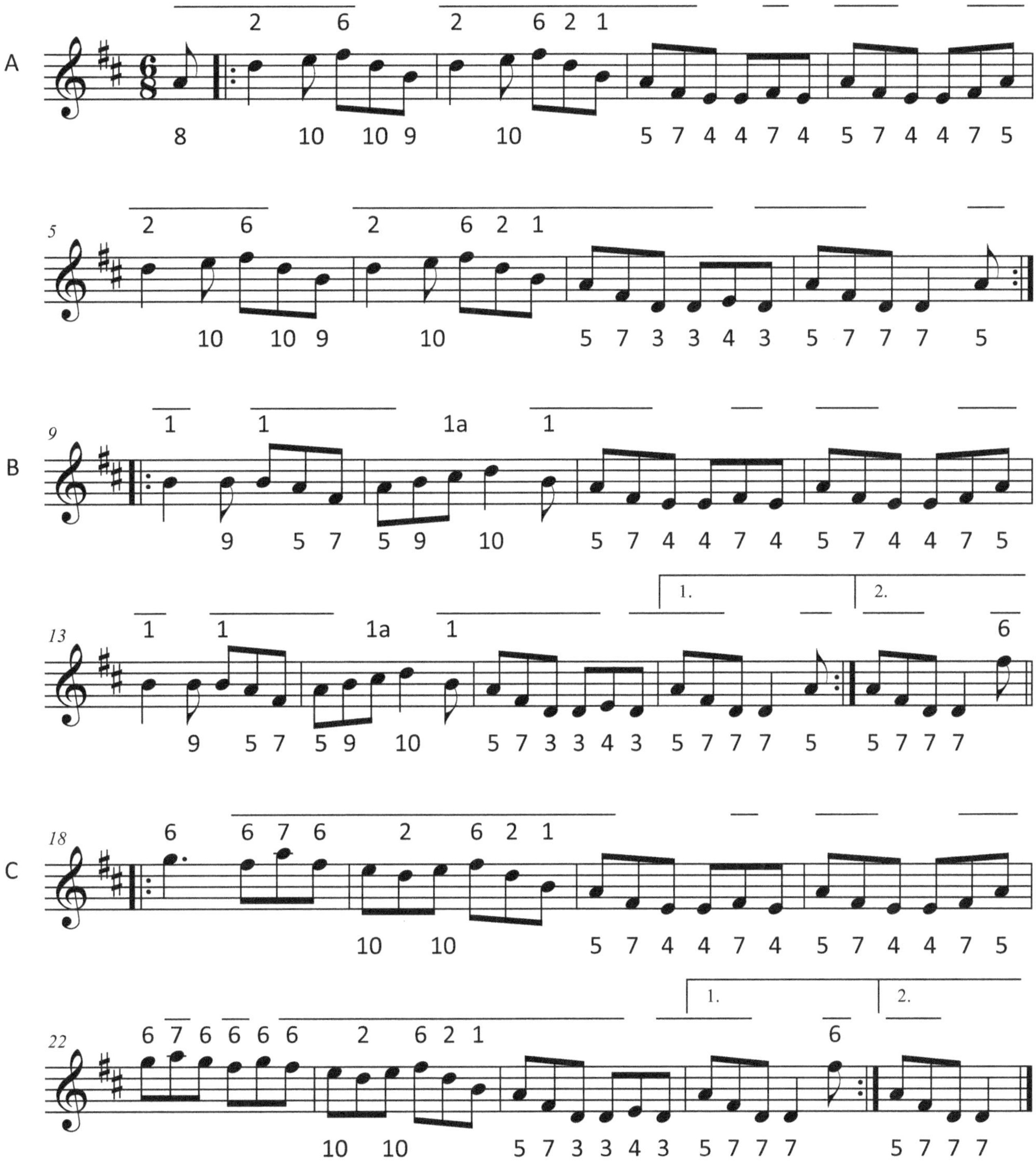

Perhaps named after the Brosna Ceili Band, this slide comes from the Sliabh Luachra area near the intersection of counties Cork, Kerry and Limerick.

Buttons played

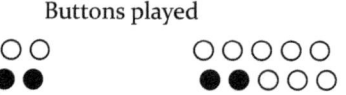

The Brosna Slide

Traditional

Named for a town in Northern Ireland, the earliest printed version is in *Kerr's Merry Melodies* dated 1886.

Buttons played

Coleraine

Dennis Murphy reportedly learned this from Seamus Ennis who called it "The Dark Girl in Blue".

Buttons played

Dennis Murphy's Slide

Traditional

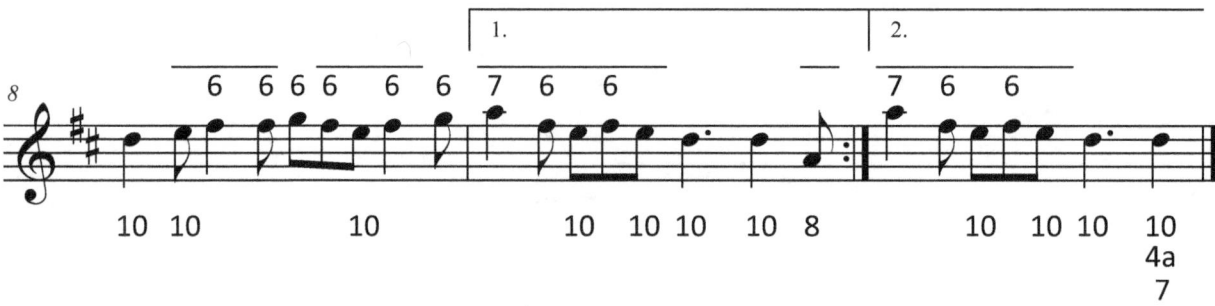

Most people know this tune from the playing (and singing) of The Chieftains.

Also known as "Cossey's Jig" where it first appeared in print in 1774. O'Neill called it "Jimmy O'Brien's Jig" and Roche calls it "Molly Brallaghan". James Morrison recorded it as "Mist on the Meadow".

Buttons played

The Maid in the Meadow

Traditional

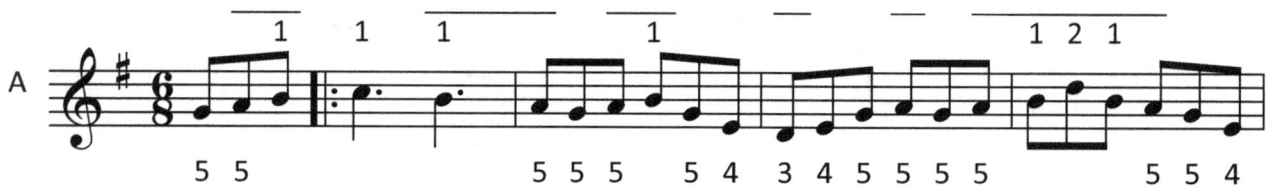

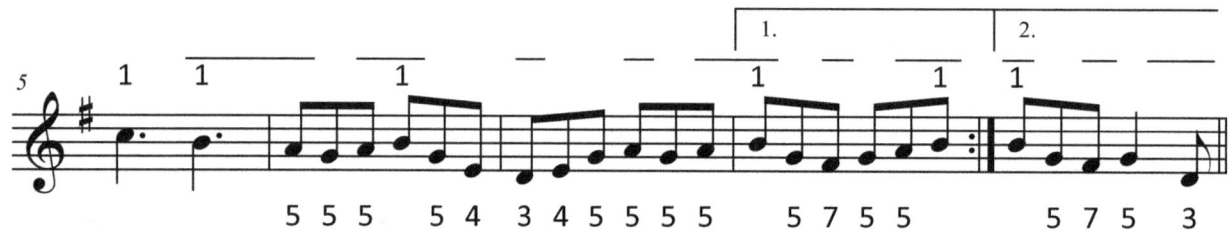

This tune was reportedly played by farmer Danny O'Keefe for Julia Clifford and Denis Murphy.

Buttons played

O'Keefe's Slide

Traditional

Learned from the concertina playing of Mandy Murray on the *Aleanna* album, this Dm Irish jig sounds especially nice when played really slowly.

Buttons played

The Orphan

Traditional

First printed in Levey's *Dance Music of Ireland* in 1858, but perhaps derived from an early march collected in Westport in County Mayo.

Buttons played

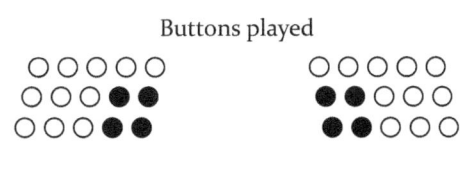

The Rakes of Kildare

Traditional

75 More Irish Session Tunes for Anglo Concertina

In O'Neills "Music of Ireland" this tune is called "The Priest's Leap", and in the Joyce Collection it is called "Down with the Tithes" and "The Widow Well-Married".

Buttons played

Saddle the Pony

Traditional

First recorded in 1924 by James Morrison and also by Peter Conlon, and in 1960 by Elizabeth Crotty. There are lots of good places for grace notes, and the B part can also be played in octaves.

Buttons played

Ship in Full Sail

Traditional

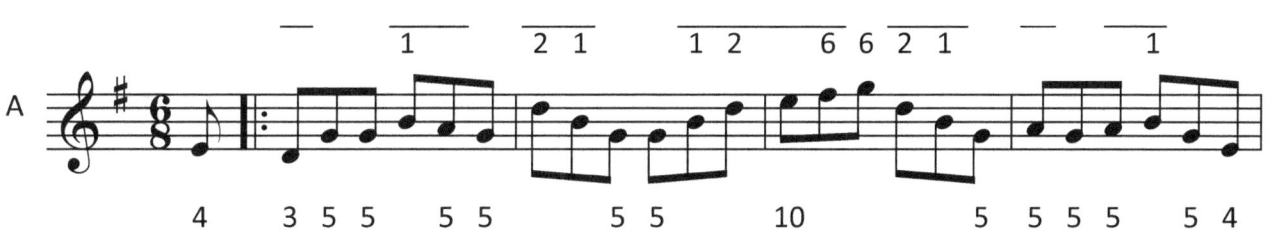

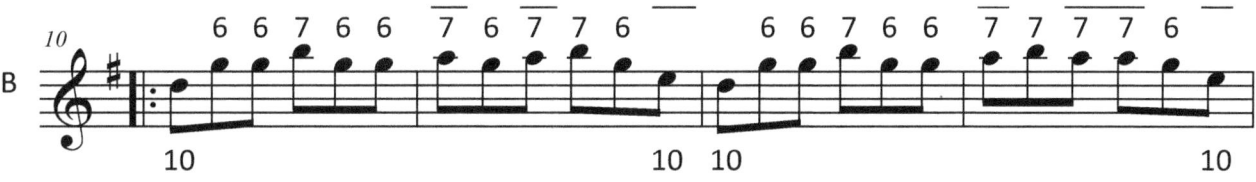

75 More Irish Session Tunes for Anglo Concertina

Also known as Airgead Réalach, The Madcap.

Buttons played

Sixpenny Money

Traditional

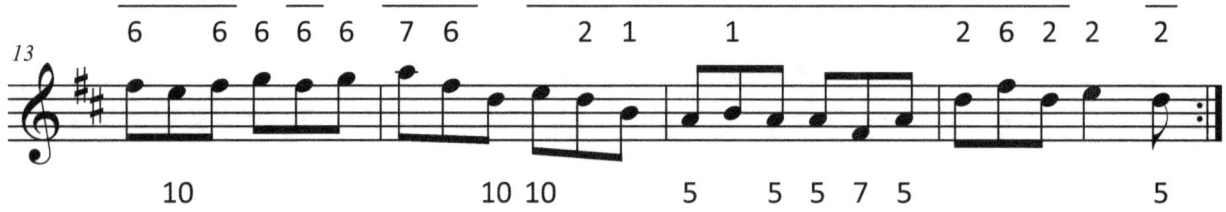

This tune is popular in Ireland, England, Shetland Islands, Prince Edward Island and America. It was first written down in England in the late 1700's.

Buttons played

Smash the Windows

Traditional

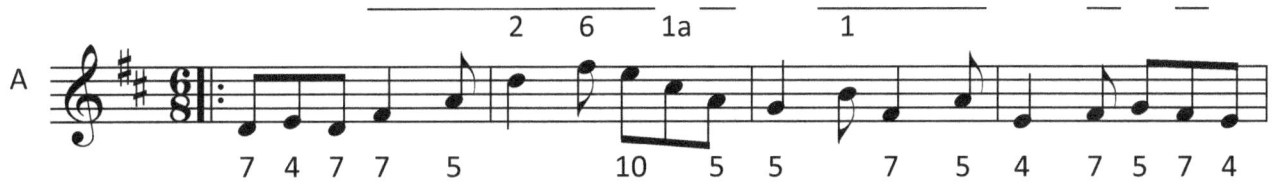

From the Slieve Luachra area in County Kerry, made famous by the 1969 album by Denis Murphy and Julia Clifford with the same title.

Buttons played

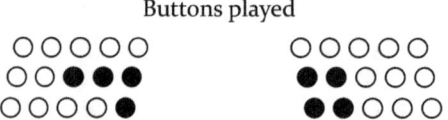

The Star Above the Garter

Traditional

Found in the 1883 *Ryans Mammoth Collection* and also called "The Dancing Master" by O'Neill.

Buttons played

Swallowtail Jig

Traditional

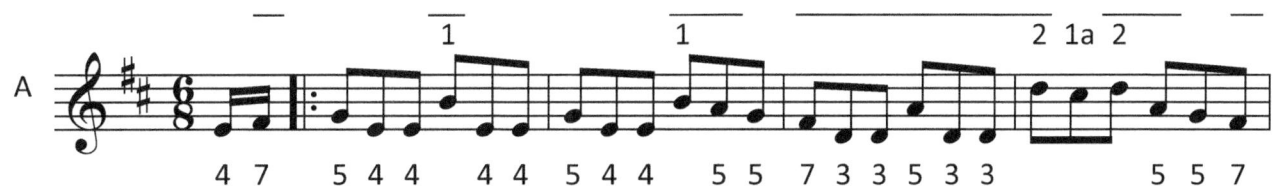

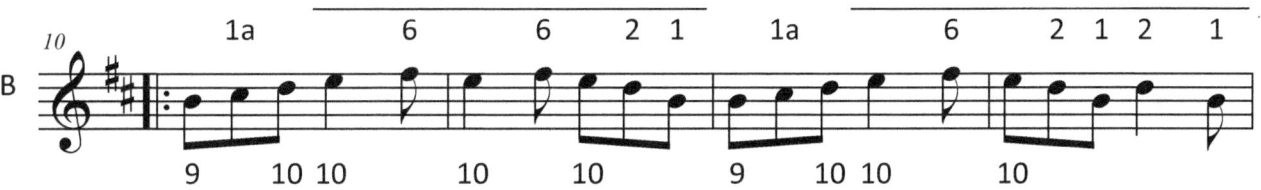

75 More Irish Session Tunes for Anglo Concertina

Called "Three Little Drummers" in O'Neill's 1903 and 1907 collections.

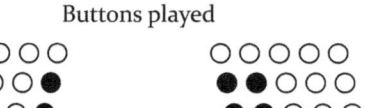

The Ten Penny Bit

Traditional

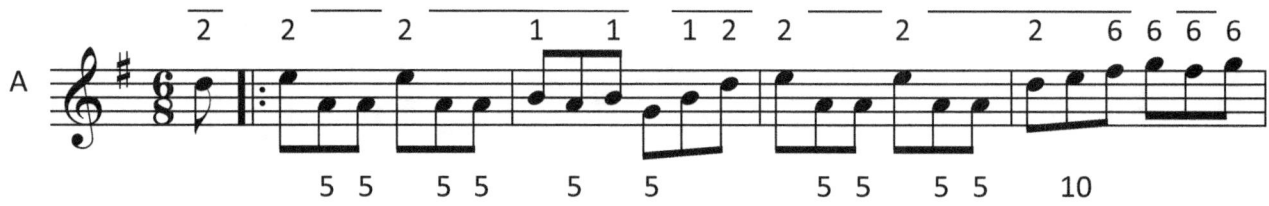

It was said that Captain O'Neill found the previous title "Pretty Young Girls For Sale" too offensive so he renamed this tune in honor of Adam Tobin, a Chicago fiddler and piper from Kilkenny.

Tobin's Favorite

Traditional

This tune is also known as "Father O'Flynn" after lyrics were added to it in 1906.

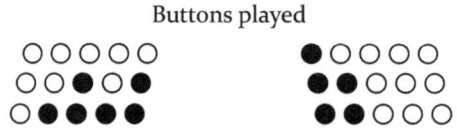

Top of Cork Road

(Father O'Flynn)

Traditional

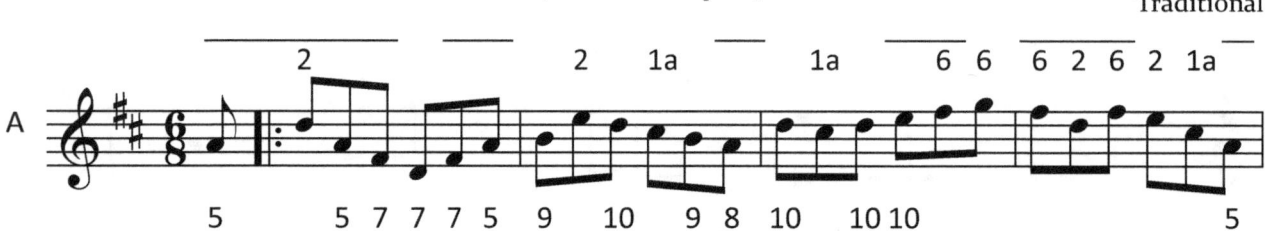

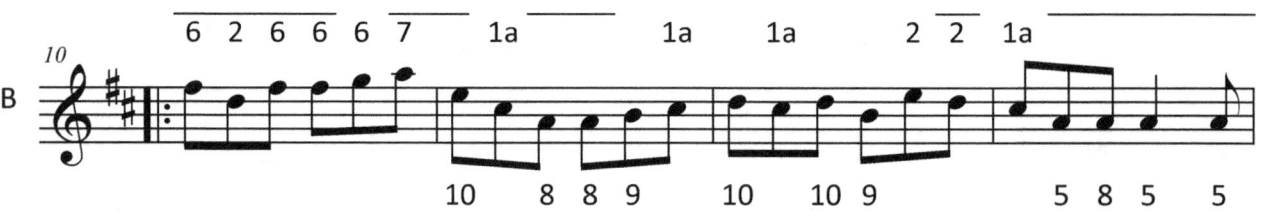

Sometimes called "The Auld/Old Lark in the Morning" and first recorded by Michael Coleman in 1927.

Trip to Sligo

Traditional

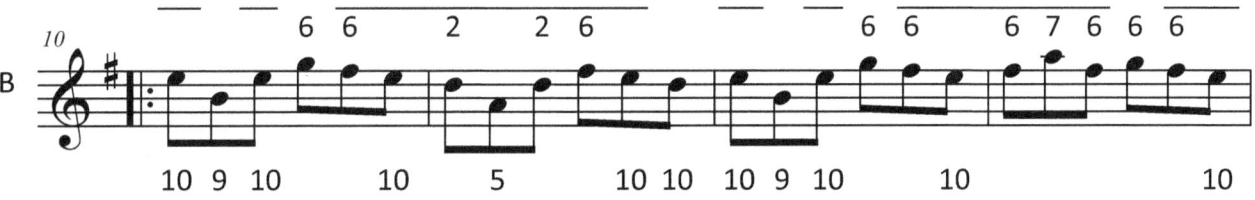

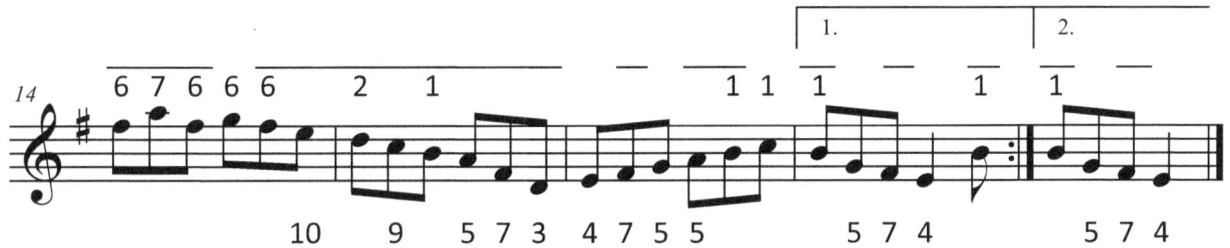

SLIP JIGS

This slip jig is popular throughout Ireland, England and Canada, and may date to the 1600's.

Buttons played

Drops of Brandy

Traditional

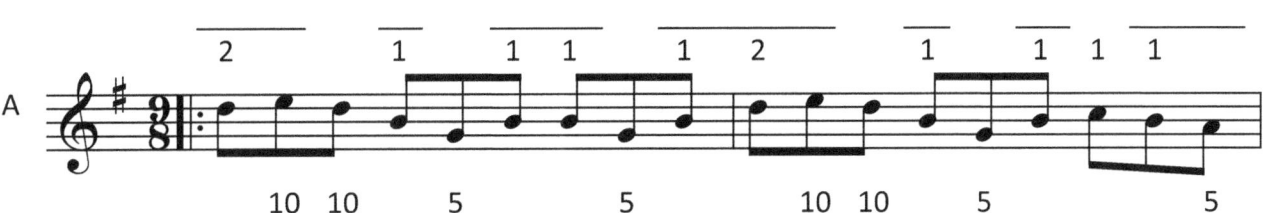

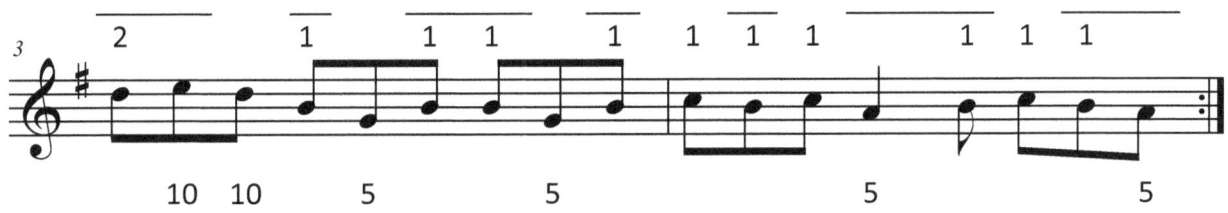

75 More Irish Session Tunes for Anglo Concertina

The title comes from Captain James Francis O'Neill, but might have been originally titled "She is Fit for a Kiss", or might mean something similar to "a penny for your thoughts". It was printed in the Petrie Collection in 1855 as "Splashing of the Churn".

A Fig for a Kiss

Traditional

75 More Irish Session Tunes for Anglo Concertina

Also known as "Nead na lachan sa mhuta", this tune was first published in 1818 and was recorded by Michael Coleman in 1925.

Buttons played

Foxhunter's Jig

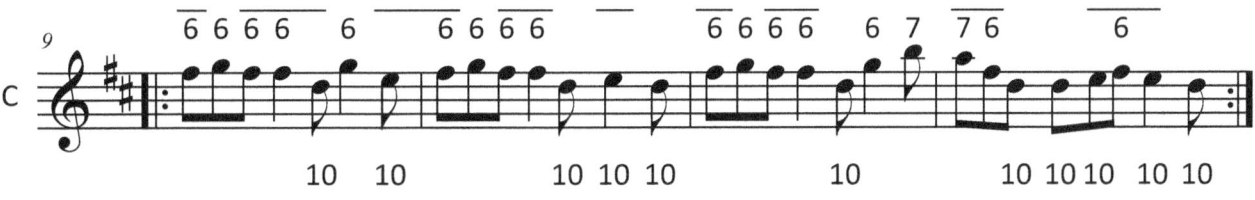

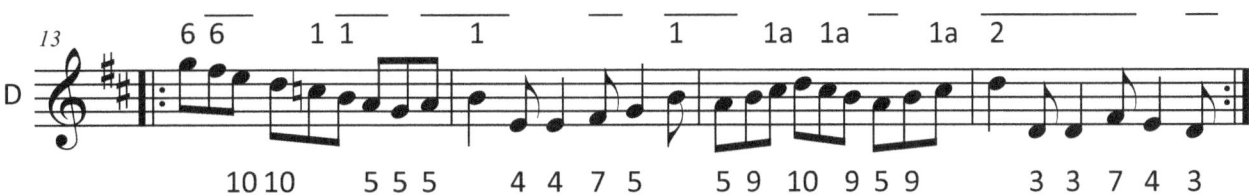

HORNPIPES

First published by O'Neill in 1903, and recorded by Michael Coleman and P.J. Dolan in 1927. Bantry Bay is off the west coast of Ireland in County Galway.

Buttons played

Bantry Bay

Traditional

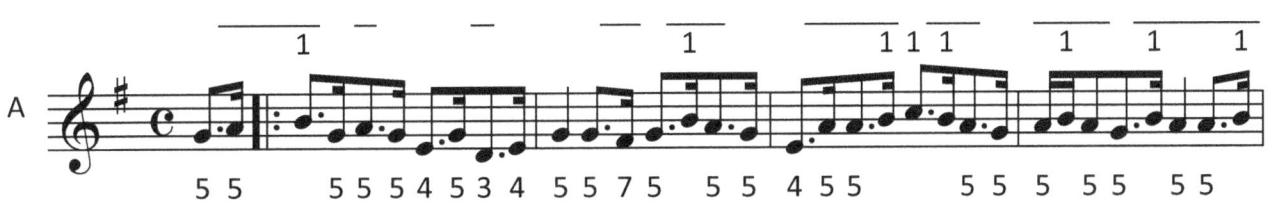

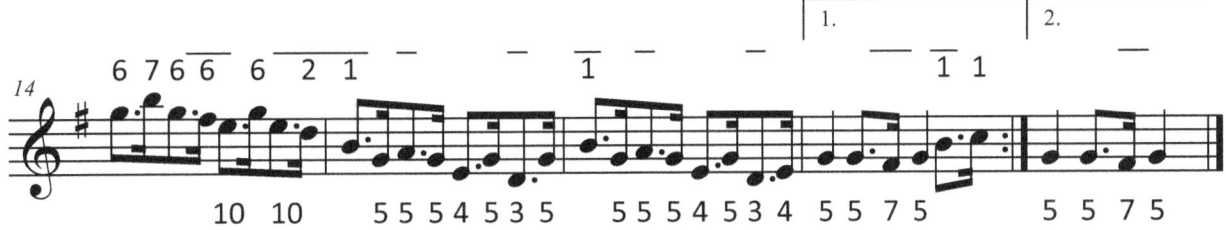

Also known as the "7th Regiment" and "Picnic Reel". First printed in the 1883 Ryan's Mammoth Collection as "Higgins' Best".

Buttons played

The Flowing Tide

Traditional

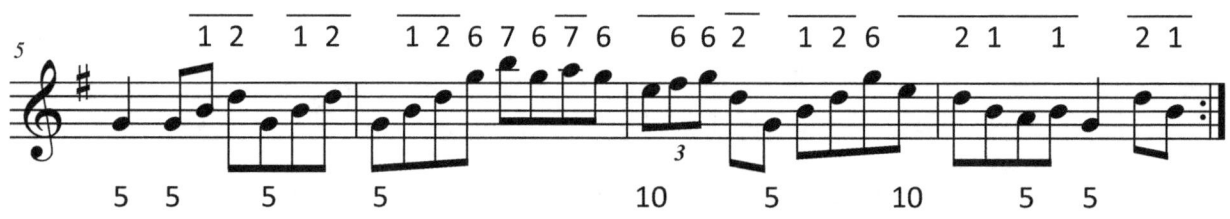

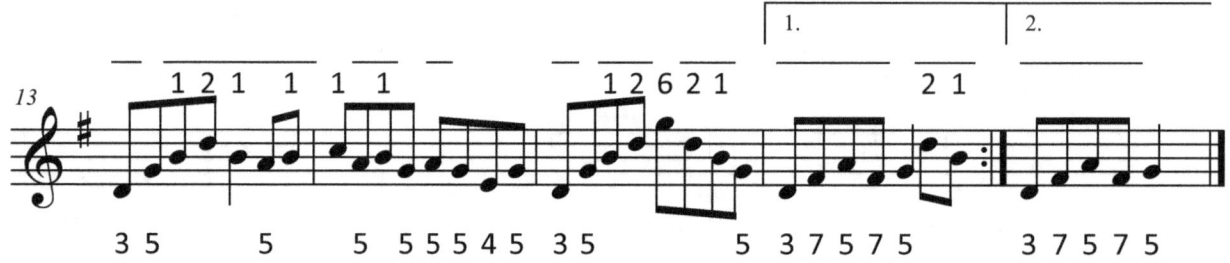

Here is how Chris Droney plays it.

Buttons played

The Flowing Tide

Traditional

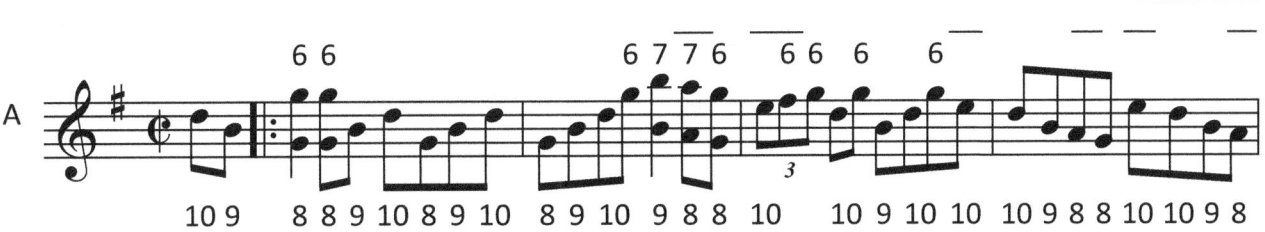

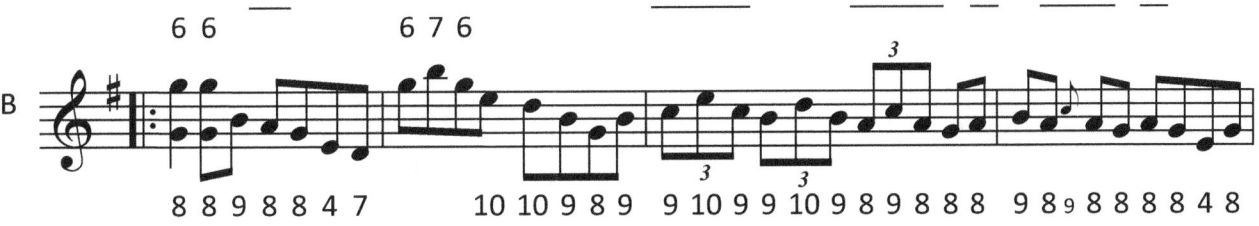

from *Chris Droney of Bell Harbour and the Tradition of the Concertina in North Clare* by Dan Worrall, Rollston Press (2022)

This hornpipe is popular in England, Scotland, Ireland, Canada and America and dates to at least the early 1800's.

Buttons played

Harvest Home

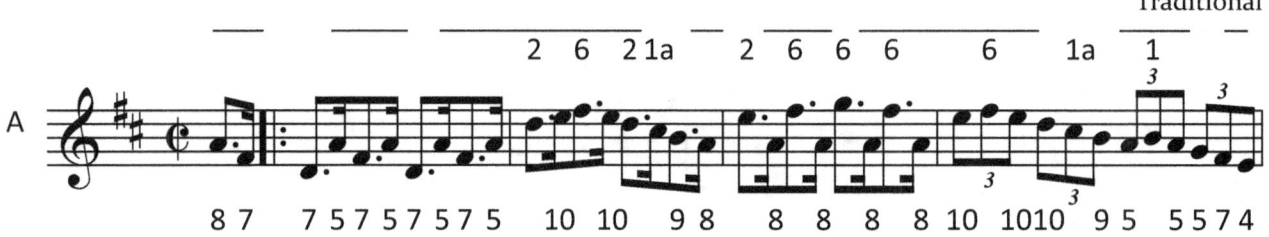

This popular hornpipe was first published in the 1903 edition of "O'Neill's Music of Ireland".

Kitty's Wedding

Traditional

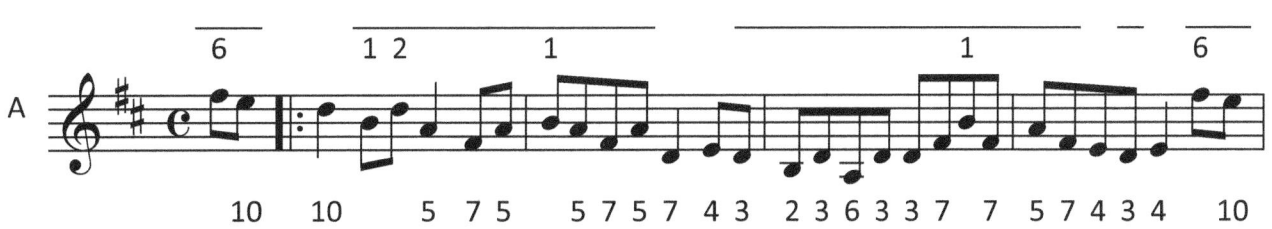

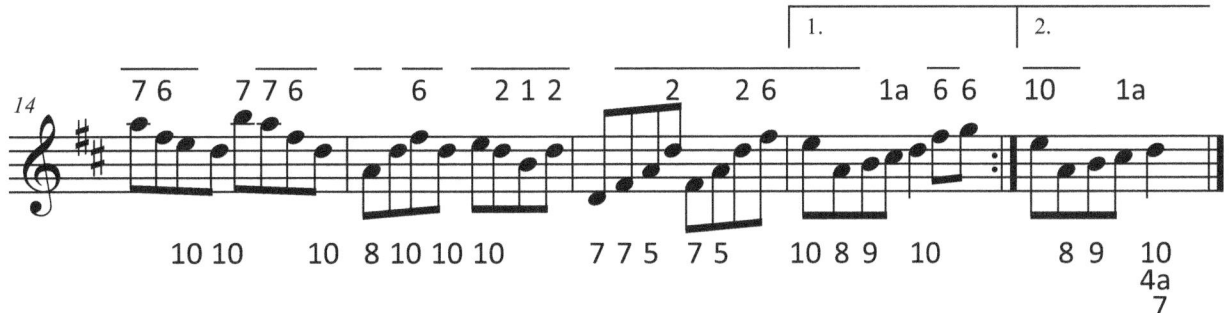

Also known as "Love Won't You Marry Me", "Johnny Won't You Marry Me", and "Some Say the Devil's Dead", and often sung as a song with a variety of different words.

Buttons played

Love Will You Marry Me?

Traditional

Popular with traditional musicians in Ireland, England and the United States, this tune was first published in the 1903 edition of O'Neill's *Music of Ireland*.

Buttons played

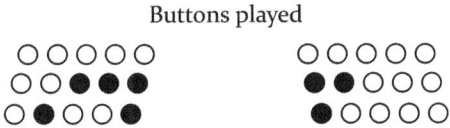

Off to California

Traditional

Transcribed from the concertina playing of Jackie Daly.

Buttons played

Walsh's Hornpipe

Traditional

POLKAS

There are three very popular polkas from Ballydesmond, a rural village beside the Blackwater River in County Cork. This one is known as #2.

Buttons played

Ballydesmond Polka #2

Traditional

75 More Irish Session Tunes for Anglo Concertina

From the playing of John Egan's son, Father Sean Egan of San Antonio, Texas.

Buttons played

John Egan's Polka

John Egan

This tune was first recorded in New York in 1936 by Sligo fiddler James Morrison who paired it with "The Magic Slipper".

Buttons played

Little Diamond

Traditional

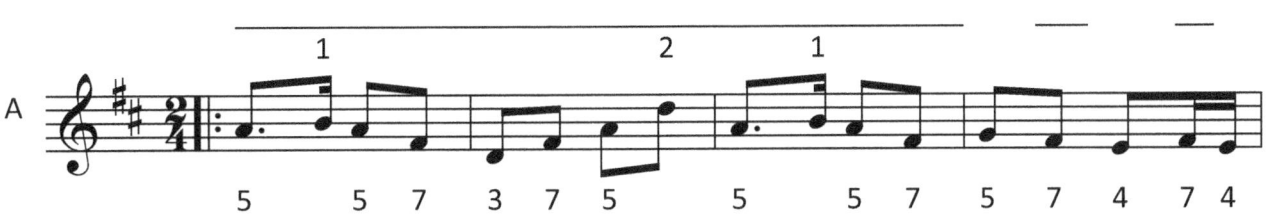

75 More Irish Session Tunes for Anglo Concertina

This tune was first published in 1909 in "Songs of the Hebrides". The words sung to this tune were added in 1935 by Johnny Bannerman for Mary McNiven.

Buttons played

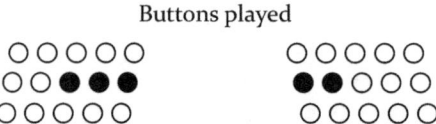

Mairi's Wedding

Traditional

Also known as the "East Limerick Polka" and sometimes "Peggy Ryan's Fancy". Murroe is a village in County Limerick.

Buttons played

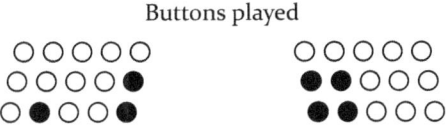

The Murroe Polka

Traditional

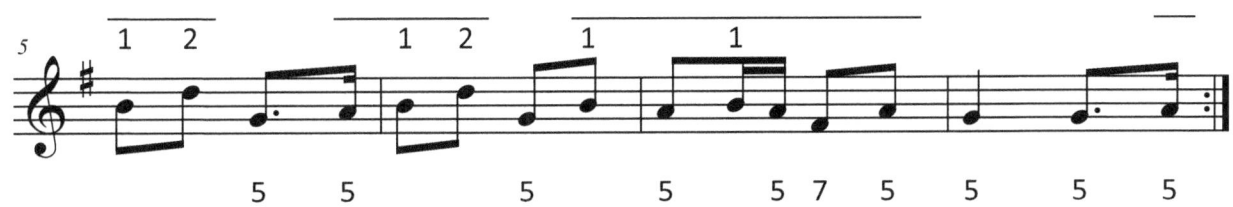

A West Kerry polka from the playing of Kerry fiddler Denis Murphy that is possibly a polka version of the Scottish strathspey "Miss Ramsay of Barnton".

Buttons played

Riding on a Load of Hay

Traditional

Named from the playing of fiddler and concertina player Terry "Cuz" Teahan who emigrated to Chicago in 1928, it is sometimes called "The Newmarket Polka".

Terry Teahan's Polka

Terry "'Cuz" Teahan

75 More Irish Session Tunes for Anglo Concertina

From the Sliabh Luachra area in County Kerry.

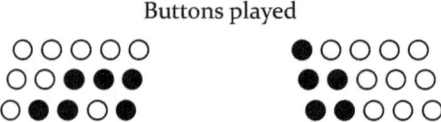

Tom Sullivan's Polka

Traditional

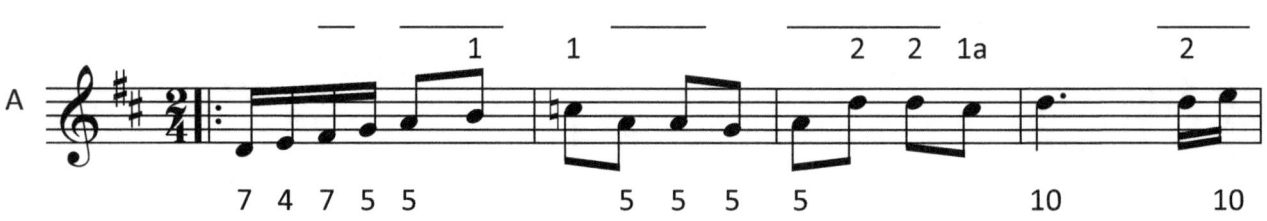

AIRS

This beautiful air was attributed to Turlough O'Carolan by William Forde in his *Encyclopedia of Melody* (c.1845). Learned from the harp playing of Bonnie Goodrich.

And here is a fairly difficult arrangement with full harmonies, with some completely different and fairly tricky fingerings. Remember to play it slowly and as expressively as possible.

Also known as "Inis Oir" this beautiful tune can be played more like a slow air in 3/4 time. Composed by Dublin button accordian player Thomas P. Walsh.

Buttons played

Inisheer

Thomas P. Walsh

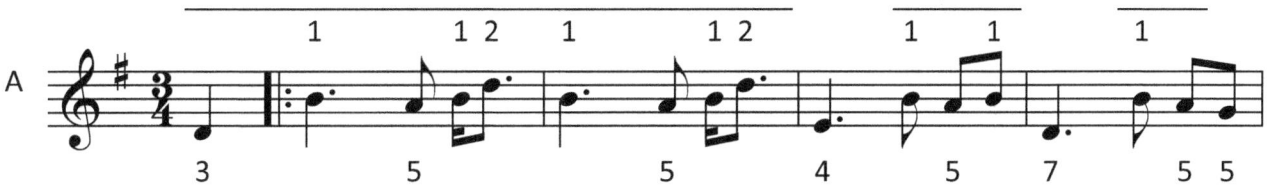

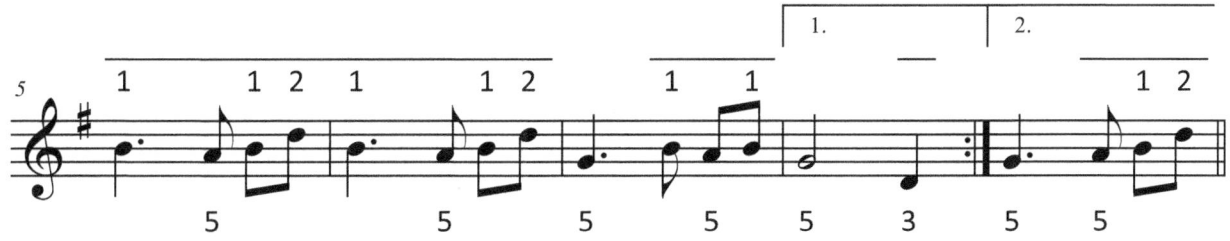

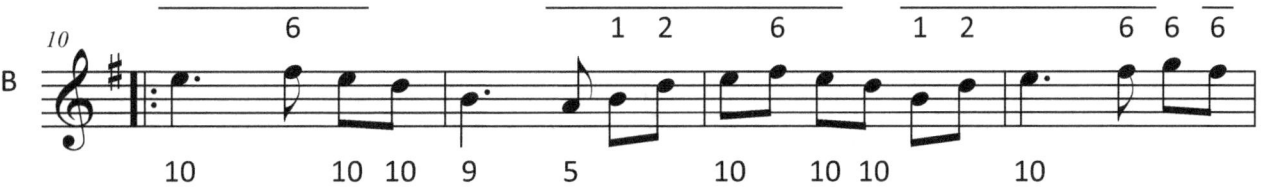

Copyright © 1975 Thomas P. Walsh / Crashed Music, used by permission

This tune was collected from a street musician in Londonderry c.1855. In 1913 English lawyer and lyricist Frederic Weatherly used this melody for his song "Danny Boy" and it has been better known by that name ever since.

Buttons played

Londonderry Air

Traditional

Known to most from the words written in 1798 by Thomas Moore, the tune is an ancient Irish melody ("The Moreen") that possibly dates to the 16th century.

The Minstrel Boy

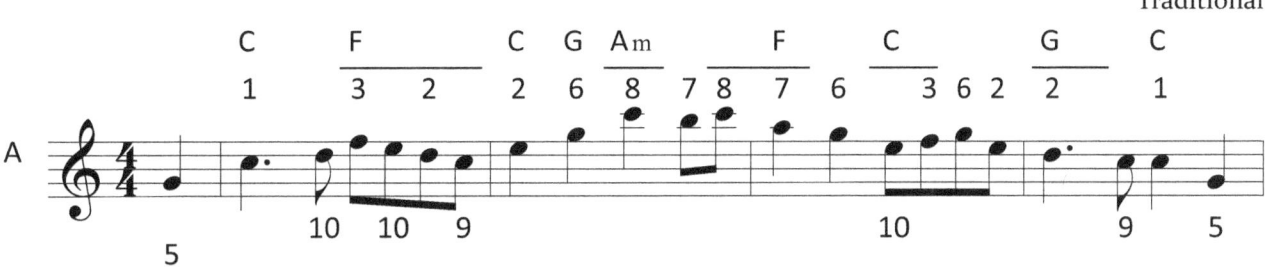

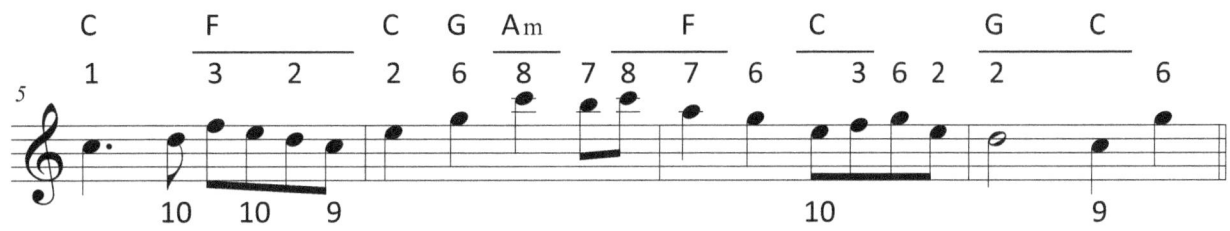

75 More Irish Session Tunes for Anglo Concertina

Also known as "Eamonn a' Chnuich", from an Irish ballad written c. 1700 in memory of Edmond O'Ryan of Knockmeill Castle, County Tipperary. With harmonies from the concertina playing of Molly Bennett.

Buttons played

Ned of the Hill

Traditional

SET DANCES, WALTZES, ETC.

This mazurka was first recorded by fiddler Hugh Gillespie in 1937.

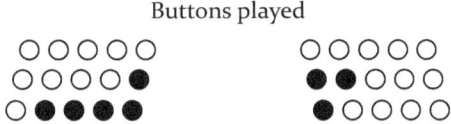

The Irish Mazurka

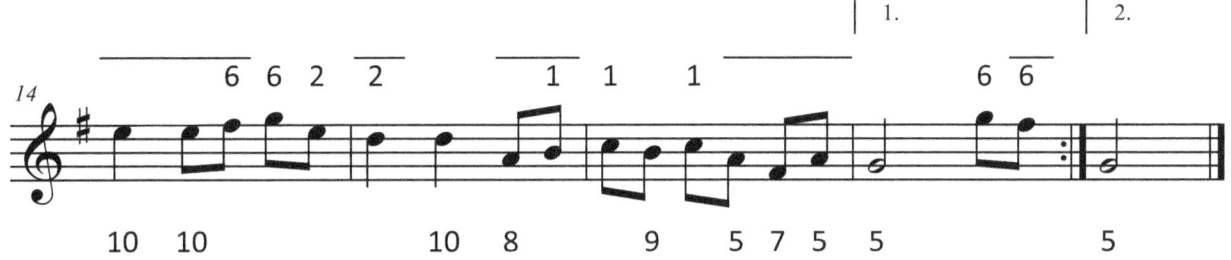

An Irish barndance named after, or perhaps from, Killavil parish in County Sligo. From the accordion playing of Jackie Daly with Arcady.

Buttons played

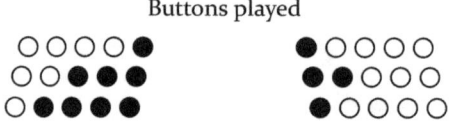

The Killavil Postman

Traditional

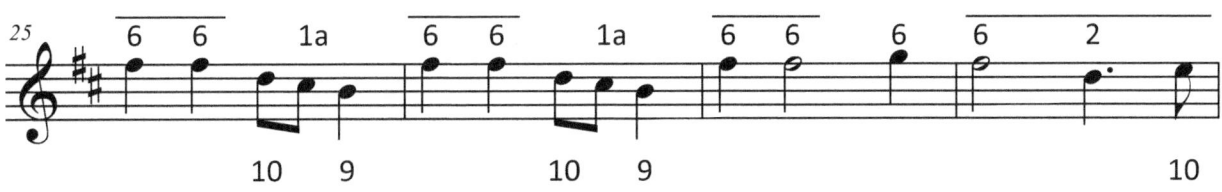

75 More Irish Session Tunes for Anglo Concertina

This tune was first recorded in 1926 by piper Leo Rowsome.

Parnell's March

Traditional

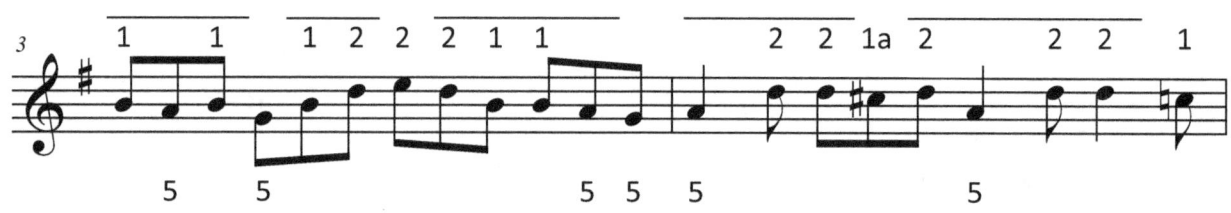

Named for either the 4th or 5th Baronet Charles Coote from County Roscommon, it was first published in Edward Bunting's *The Ancient Music of Ireland* in 1840.

Buttons played

Planxty Charles Coote

Turlough O'Carolan (1670-1738)

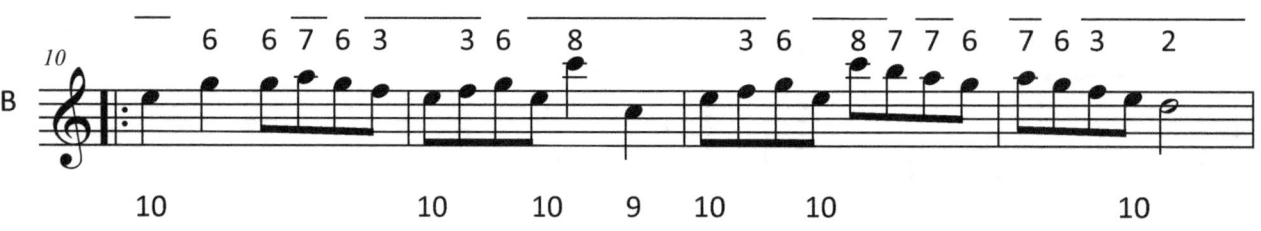

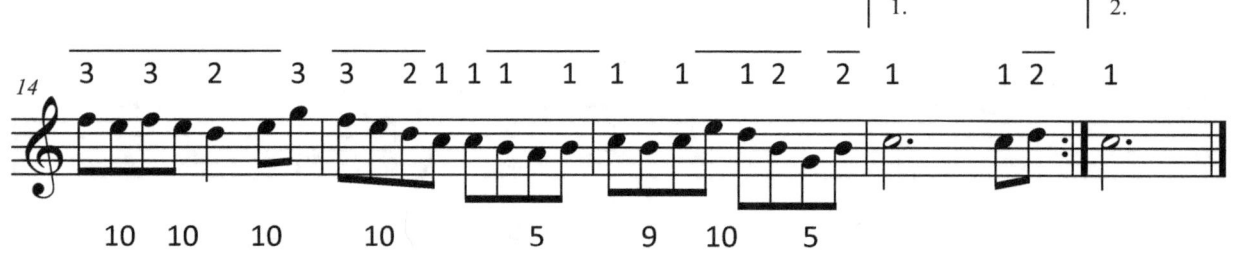

Composed in the early 1700's by legendary Irish harper Turlough O'Carolan and named for Colonel John Irwin of Tanrego House on Ballysodare Bay in County Sligo.

Buttons played

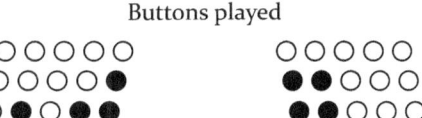

Planxty Irwin

Turlough O'Carolan (1670-1738)

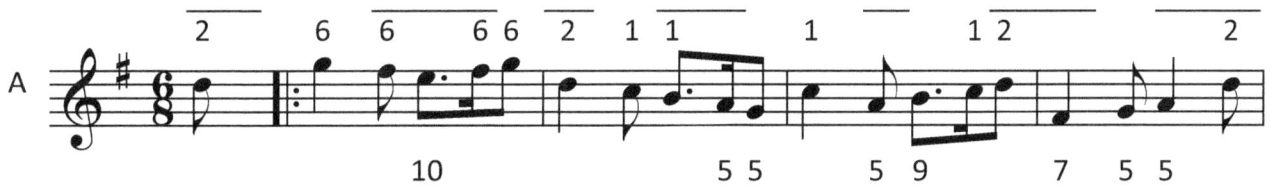

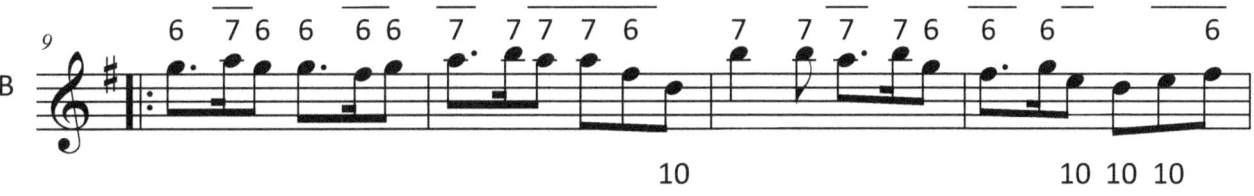

This lovely tune was written in the 1700's by Donal MacNamara from County Mayo.

Buttons played

The South Wind

Donal MacNamara

THE AUTHORS

Gary Coover began playing the concertina soon after discovering British and Irish traditional music while in college, inspired by the music of Steeleye Span and concertina playing of John Kirkpatrick and John Watcham.

In 2013 he published his first Anglo instruction book, *Anglo Concertina in the Harmonic Style*, which included tunes from William Kimber, John Kirkpatrick, Jody Kruskal, Bertram Levy, Kenneth Loveless, Brian Peters, Andy Turner, and many others.

The success of this book led to the creation of Rollston Press, which today has nearly 40 titles in its catalog, over half of which are instruction books for a wide variety of music especially arranged for the Anglo concertina.

All of Gary's books utilize a simple and popular "play-by-number" tablature system based on 19th century Anglo tutors. Most of the books also feature video instruction – Rollston Press was the first music publisher to incorporate QR codes that link to YouTube videos and SoundCloud audio recordings.

Ernestine Healy is from County Mayo and is an internationally recognized concertina player, as well as a tutor and producer on the Irish musical scene. She has been engaged for events such as the 'Milwaukee Irish Music Festival', workshops in Germany, 'Tocane' in France, Music Generation Traditional Festival in Borris Carlow, 'Scoil Eigse' as part of the All Ireland Fleadh, Consairtín, 'Eigse Mrs.Crotty' in Kilrush, Co Clare, Corofin Traditional Festival, as well as numerous other festivals & workshops around Ireland, Europe & America.

She has worked as a lecturer in the Irish World Academy of Music and Dance, in the University of Limerick. Having occupied the position of Acting Course Director on the Graduate Diploma in Music Education postgrad programme during 2008/09, she then went onto lecture on the BA in Irish Music and Dance undergraduate programme in 2009. Ernestine has also worked as a tutor in the School of Music at the University College Cork.

In addition to being an engaging performer and teacher, Ernestine's portfolio also extends to research on Irish traditional music, Composition & Music Education for which she was duly awarded a First class Masters degree from the University of Limerick in 2008. Ernestine is one of the concertina tutors with OAIM (Online Academy of Irish Music).

Ernestine is a regular performer on both local and national radio, and has made numerous TV appearances including 'The Fleadh Programme' & 'The Reel Deal' & was a featured performer on the concertina edition of Mná an Cheoil (Tg4 2016), and her Meitheal suites have been performed at Dublin's National Concert Hall and on TG4's Fleadh 2023.'

www.ernestinehealy.com

ALPHABETICAL LIST OF TUNES

Tune	Page
Ashplant, The	11
Ballydesmond #2	75
Bank of Ireland	12
Bantry Bay	65
Behind the Haystack	43
Blind Mary (Mhaire Dhall)	91, 92
Brosna Slide	44
Castle Kelly	13
Coleraine	45
Concertina Reel	14
Cup of Tea	15
Dennis Murphy's Slide	46
Dingle Regatta	47
Drops of Brandy	85
Farewell to Ireland	16
Fig for a Kiss	86
Flowing Tide, The	66, 67
Foxhunter's Jig	87
Glass of Beer	18
Green Fields of America	19
Harvest Home	68
High Reel	20
Humours of Tulla	21
Inisheer	93
Irish Mazurka, The	99
John Egan's	76
Killavil Postman	100
Kitty's Wedding	69
Little Diamond	77
Londonderry Air	94
Love Will You Marry Me	70
Maid in the Meadow	48
Maid of Mount Kisco	22
Mairi's Wedding	78
Minstrel Boy	95
Miss Monaghan	23
Morning Dew	24
Murroe Polka	79
Music in the Glen	25
Musical Priest	26
Ned of the Hill	96
O'Keefe's Slide	49
Off to California	71
Old Concertina Reel	27
Old Torn Petticoat	28
Orphan, The	50
Over the Moor to Maggie	29
Paddy Fahey's #1	30
Parnell's March	102
Pigeon on the Gate	31
Planxty Charles Coote	104
Planxty Irwin	105
Rakes of Kildare	51
Rakish Paddy	32
Riding on a Load of Hay	80
Saddle the Pony	52
Scholar, The	33
Ship in Full Sail	53
Ships Are Sailing	34
Silver Spire	35
Sixpenny Money	54
Smash the Windows	55
South Wind	106
St. Anne's Reel	36
Star Above the Garter	56
Star of Munster	37
Swallowtail Jig	57
Swallowtail Reel	38
Swinging on a Gate	39
Tenpenny Bit	58
Terry Teahan's	81
Tobin's Favorite	59
Tom Sullivan's	82
Top of Cork Road (Father O'Flynn)	60
Trip to Sligo	61
Walsh's Hornpipe	72

ROLLSTON PRESS
ANGLO CONCERTINA BOOKS

Anglo Concertina in the Harmonic Style

Easy Anglo 1-2-3

Christmas Concertina

Civil War Concertina

75 Irish Session Tunes for Anglo Concertina

Pirate Songs for Concertina

Sailor Songs for Concertina

Sea Songs for 20-Button Anglo Concertina

Cowboy Concertina

A Garden of Dainty Delights

The Jeffries Duet Concertina Tutor

The Anglo Concertina Music of John Watcham

The Anglo Concertina Music of John Kirkpatrick

The Anglo Concertina Music of Phil Ham

Anglo Concertina from Beginner to Master

Chris Droney of Bell Harbour

86 Swiss and German Folksongs for Anglo Concertina

The Anglo Concertina Handbook of Tunes and Methods for Irish Traditional Music

19th Century Anglo

75 *More* Irish Session Tunes for Anglo Concertina

*Available from Amazon,
McNeela Music, Red Cow Music, and other fine retailers*

www.ingramcontent.com/pod-product-compliance
Lightning Source LLC
Chambersburg PA
CBHW080553230426
43663CB00015B/2824